Cookies

The Top 100 Most Delicious Cookie Recipes

By Ace McCloud
Copyright © 2015

Disclaimer

The information provided in this book is designed to provide helpful information on the subjects discussed. This book is not meant to be used, nor should it be used, to diagnose or treat any medical condition. For diagnosis or treatment of any medical problem, consult your own physician. The publisher and author are not responsible for any specific health or allergy needs that may require medical supervision and are not liable for any damages or negative consequences from any treatment, action, application or preparation, to any person reading or following the information in this book. Any references included are provided for informational purposes only. Readers should be aware that any websites or links listed in this book may change.

Table of Contents

Introduction 6
Chapter 1: Short History of Cookies and Equipment Needed 8
Chapter 2: Delicious Bar Cookies 11
Chapter 3: Mouth Watering Drop Cookies 24
Chapter 4: Rolled Cookies Everyone Will Love 44
Chapter 5: Excellent Filled and Sandwich Cookies 58
Chapter 6: No Bake Cookies that Taste Great 72
Chapter 7: Special Occasion Cookies 81
Conclusion 100
My Other Books and Audio Books 101

Be sure to check out my website for all my Books and Audio books.

www.AcesEbooks.com

Introduction

I want to thank you and congratulate you for buying the book, "Cookies: The Top 100 Most Delicious Cookie Recipes."

This book contains proven steps and delicious recipes for making mouthwatering cookies your family and friends will love!

Remember way back in your childhood and came home after school to find that Mom had put out a little snack consisting of cookies and milk, or do you remember getting caught with your hand in the cookie jar. I don't know about you, but I thought my mom made the best cookies and she had eyes in the back of her head. I know now she had an arsenal of cookie recipes passed down from generations and from clippings of magazines and she could always hear that little "clink" sound when the cookie jar lid slid down no matter how careful I was.

Not many kids these days know the joy and delights of home backed cookies. You go to the store, peruse the cookie aisle filled with colorful packages with elves and other creatures on the label, and bring home sweet treats filled with preservatives that enable these cookies to stay fresh for months. They usually don't last for months because they are eaten before their shelf life expires, so why do they need all those preservatives.

If you make your own cookies, you also have a preservative. It is called the freezer. Just put fresh baked cookies or cookie dough in freezer bags and take them out when you need them. You will always have fresh cookies that do not contain things you can't even pronounce.

Cookies are easy to make. You can make a few or dozens. They might take a little bit of time and effort, but the results are a great tasting cookie without added chemicals. They are usually cheaper to make than they are to buy. You also put love into cookies when you back them yourself. Your family knows you love them because you took the time and effort to make the sweet treat yourself.

This book has 100 cookies recipes and I've only skimmed the surface of cookie baking. There are millions of recipes out there and they come from all over the world. These recipes are the most common types and the ones I know are delicious. They are separated into categories including bars, drop cookies, rolled cookies, filled, and sandwich cookies, no bake cookies and special occasion cookies. There is a bonus first chapter about the history of cookies and equipment you need to make them properly.

Have fun experimenting with these recipes. The reason there are so many cookie recipes out there in the world is because they are easily changed. I have added variations to many of these recipes, but you should try to customize them yourself. Make your recipes personal to delight your family with their own favorite flavors.

Chapter 1: Short History of Cookies and Equipment Needed

Cookies have been a sweet snack for centuries, but early cookies bear little resemblance to the types of cookies we have today. Cookies are defined as a flour and sugar based small cake eaten with the hands. Cookies have different names today. In England they may ask you if you would like a biscuit. Instead of a soft muffin like object made with baking soda that Americans think of as a biscuit, you will get a sweet cookie. In Spain and other Spanish speaking countries galletas are cookies and in Germany they may be called keks. The Dutch call them koekje and Italians may refer to them as amaretti or biscotti.

A cookie by any other name would taste as sweet, to paraphrase Shakespeare. In the seventh century in what is now Iran, they made their appearance. You need sugar to make a proper cookie and this is where sugar can is thought to have originated. In 510 BC soldiers found reeds that tasted sweet. They thought it odd to have no bees because they believed the sweetness in the reeds was honey. Alexander the Great is credited with the spread of sugar to the Mediterranean around 327 BC. By the time of the Renaissance, cookbooks were filled with cookie recipes.

Cookies were first used to test ovens way back when ovens did not have thermometers or temperatures you could set. Ovens were fueled by wood or coal fires. These little sweet cakes were popped in the oven before other baked goods to make sure the oven was either hot enough or not too hot. It didn't take long for someone to figure out these little hand held cakes were pretty good and should become a regular food.

Immigrants to the United States from Scotland, England and Holland (remember the Puritans) brought cookie recipes with them. They may have been strict, but loved their sweets. Tea was popular in that culture and cookies were often called tea cakes in high society. Cookies became a favorite snack and each region in the US made them different. People in the south may use citrus, coconut or nuts while those in the north stuck to butter and chocolate they had shipped in.

There is a science to baking cookies and you can learn more about that by watching the YouTube Video "The Chemistry of Cookies" by Stephanie Warren.

EQUIPMENT NEEDED

Some equipment is needed to bake cookies effectively.

Basics:

1. **Measuring Cups** – either glass or plastic as long as you have 1 cup down to 1/4 cup.

2. **Measuring Spoons** – either metal or plastic as long as you have 1 Tablespoon down to 1/8 teaspoon.

3. **Spatula** – This usually has a wooden or plastic handle and a soft plastic or rubber end that can scrape the sides of the bowl and get all the cookie dough down and combined together.

4. **Oven Mitts** – These are a must so you do not burn your hands when you remove the cookies from the oven.

5. **Bakeware** – You will need flat cookie sheets for some cookies and cake pans in metal or glass for others. Cookie sheets come in a variety of types and sizes. There are the non-stick ones and just plain metal sheets. It doesn't matter which one you choose because you always use parchment paper so that your cookie bottoms don't get too brown. Check the YouTube video called "Baking Sheet Characteristics for Perfect Cookies" from Better Homes and Gardens Kitchen that explains how to use cookie sheets and the best ones to use.

6. **Parchment paper** – You can get parchment paper on rolls in your grocery store where you would purchase foil. You can check out the YouTube video called "How to Use Parchment Paper" by Sue Walker for great information on how to use parchment paper to make cookies.

7. **Non-stick spray** – You will want to use this when making a bar recipe. If you don't the cookies will stick to the sides and bottom and it will be impossible to get them out.

8. **Cooling racks** – These are a nice thing to have. They are metal racks that are mesh or have small bars and spaces going across them to let air completely surround the finished cookie and help it to cool quickly. You don't really have to have cooling racks. You can just let the cookies sit on newspaper or wax paper until they cool, but cooling racks are a bit more sanitary.

9. **Mixer** – You should have a mixer because it is difficult to mix cookie batter by hand. It is usually very thick and you can't get all the ingredients combined well stirring by hand.

10. **Rolling pin** – If you want to make rolled cookies, you need a rolling pin. I like the wooden kind and you can get cloth coverings for them if you want. I find if you flour your dough well you don't need it.

11. **Cookie cutters** – If you want to make cut out cookies, you will need cookie cutters. They come in a variety of shapes and sizes and can be plastic or metal. Make sure they have a sharp edge for easy cutting.

From animal crackers to fancy lady locks, cookies are a favorite treat almost everywhere in the world.

Chapter 2: Delicious Bar Cookies

Bar cookies are probably the easiest to make. You don't have to roll them, assemble them or anything else. You just bake them in a pan and when they are cool, cut them into squares or bars. Bar cookies come in a variety of flavors and some are cake like while others are more dense and chewy. Brownies are probably the most popular bar cookie.

BROWNIES

The name of this cookie comes from the color of the cookie after they are baked. They are either cake-like or chewing and gooey and chocolate. You don't have to have a mixer to make these as you can hand stir the ingredients. The batter isn't all that thick. This makes about 16 bars.

Ingredients:
1/2 cup butter
1 cup granulated sugar
2 beaten eggs
1-1/4 teaspoon vanilla
1/3 cup unsweetened cocoa powder
1/2 cup all-purpose flour
1/4 teaspoon salt
1/4 teaspoon baking powder
For the Frosting:
3 tablespoons softened butter
3 tablespoons unsweetened cocoa powder
1 tablespoon honey
1-1/4 teaspoon vanilla
1 cup confectioners' sugar

Directions:
Preheat your oven to 350 degrees F and spray an 8 inch square pan with non-stick spray.

Melt the butter in a large saucepan over low heat. Once it is melted remove the pan from the heat and stir in the sugar, eggs, and vanilla. Stir with a spatula until it is well combined and add the cocoa, flour, salt, and baking powder. Once combined well with just a few little lumps, scoop into the baking pan. Place in the oven and bake for 25 to 30 minutes. The center should not wiggle when shaken and the sides should be pulling away from the pan. You can't use the toothpick method here because brownies never let the toothpick come out clean. If the toothpick is clean, the brownies are overcooked. Let the brownies cool. You can eat them as is or frost them with the frosting below.

In a mixing bowl combine all the ingredients and mix on high until smooth and creamy. Frost brownies when they are still just slightly warm. This will enable the frosting to sink in and melt slightly and become glossy.

Variations: You can add 3/4 cup of chocolate chips or 3/4 to 1 cup chopped nuts to the brownie mix and bake as directed or place half the batter in the pan, top with unwrapped chocolate peppermint patties and cover with the rest of the batter and bake.

BUTTERSCOTCH BLONDIES

Blondies are also considered a form of brownies and get their name from their color too. They are usually a non-chocolate brownie with butterscotch chips or nuts. This recipe makes about 3 to 4 dozen depending on how big you cut them.

Ingredients:
2-1/2 cups all-purpose flour
1/4 teaspoon salt
1 teaspoon baking powder
1 cup shortening
1-3/4 cup brown sugar that is packed
2 beaten large eggs
1 teaspoon vanilla
1-2/3 cups or 11 oz package of butterscotch flavored chips

Directions:
Preheat your oven to 350 degrees F and spray a 13 x 9 inch pan with non-stick spray.

Whisk together the flour, salt and baking powder, and set aside. Place the shortening, brown sugar, eggs and vanilla in the bowl of your mixer and beat until smooth. Add the dry mixture to the shortening mixture in the mixer until it is all combined. Remove from the mixer and fold the butterscotch chips in by hand.

Pour the batter into the prepared pan and bake for 30 to 40 minutes or until the blondies start to pull away from the sides of the pan and the center is firm. Cool and cut into bars or squares.

Variations: Use chocolate chips instead of butterscotch chips or combine half and half. You can also add 1/2 to 3/4 cup of chopped nuts with the chips or alone.

DATE BARS

This is an old recipe from way back. The crust is made from rolled oats and filled with sweet dates. This recipe makes about 12 bars so you might want to make 2 pans.

Ingredients:
1-1/2 cups rolled oats (Old Fashioned, not Quick Cooking)
1-1/2 cups flour
1/4 teaspoon salt
1/2 teaspoon baking soda
1 cup brown sugar, packed tight
3/4 cup softened butter
3/4 pound pitted dates that have been diced
1 cup water
1/3 cup brown sugar, packed in addition to the one above
1 teaspoon lemon juice

Directions:
Preheat the oven to 350 degrees F and spray the bottom of a 9 inch square baking pan.

Mix together the rolled oats, flour, salt and 1 cup of brown sugar in a large bowl and whisk it with a wire whisk until it is well combined. Cut the butter in with a pie crust cutter until the mixture looks crumbly and well combined. Press half of this mixture into the bottom of the 9 inch square pan.

Place the dates, water, and 1/3 cup of brown sugar in a medium saucepan over medium heat. Bring this mixture to a boil and cook, stirring constantly until it thickens well. Add the lemon juice and remove from heat. Spread this mixture onto the crust and top with the rest of the crumbled oat mixture.

Bake for 20 to 25 minutes or until the top is lightly toasted. Cool and cut into squares for a gooey and delicious treat.

Variation: Instead of using lemon juice us 1 teaspoon 1 teaspoon of almond extract. It gives the cookie a different and delightful flavor.

CHOCOATE CHIP BARS

If you want chocolate chip cookies and don't have the time to form each cookie, this bar recipe still has the flavor without all the trouble. The cookie is crisp on the outside and soft inside and will be a favorite in your house. At Christmas I sprinkle the pans with red and green sugar before baking to dress them up for the holiday. This recipe makes about 3 to 4 dozen bars

Ingredients:
2 -1/4 cups all-purpose flour
1 teaspoon baking soda

1/2 teaspoon salt
1 cup shortening
3/4 cup granulated sugar
3/4 cup brown sugar that is tightly packed
1-1/4 teaspoon vanilla
2 large eggs
1 – 12 oz packages semi-sweet chocolate chips

Directions:
Preheat the oven to 375 degrees F and prepare a 9 by 13 inch baking dish with non-stick spray on the bottom.

Combine the flour, baking soda and salt in a large bowl. Whisk with a wire whisk until completely combined and set aside. Place the shortening and both sugars in a mixing bowl and beat until smooth and creamy. Add the vanilla and eggs and beat until smooth. Gradually add the dry ingredients to the ingredients in the mixer until it is all well combined. Remove the bowl from the mixer and hand mix in the chocolate chips.

Scrape the batter into the baking dish and bake for 30 to 45 minutes or until the cookie edges begin to pull away from the pan and the center is firm. Remove from the oven and cool, and then cut into squares or bars.

It sometimes takes a little longer for these bar cookies to cook so if the middle seems to be a little fluid, let them cook longer, just watch so the edges don't burn. The cookies should be a light golden brown when they are done. These bar cookies are also very thick. If you want a thinner cookie use a jelly roll pan and only cook for about 20 minutes.

Variations: Add 3/4 cup chopped nuts to the cookies or instead of chocolate chips, use chocolate chunks.

PEANUT BUTTER BALLS

Anyone who likes peanut butter will love these cookies. I don't particularly like peanut butter, but these cookies taste pretty good to me. There are just a few ingredients and they make about 2 dozen bars depending on how big you cut them.

Ingredients:
1-1/2 cups all-purpose flour
1 teaspoon baking soda
1/2 cup rolled oats (the Old Fashion, not Quick oats)
1/8 teaspoon salt
1/2 cup shortening
1 cup brown sugar packed tight

3/4 cup smooth peanut butter
1 egg
1 teaspoon vanilla
3/4 cup chopped peanuts

Directions:
Preheat oven to 350 degrees F and spray the bottom of a 9 x 13 inch pan with non-stick spray. HINT: The reason some recipes say to only spray the bottom of the pan is that if you spray the sides, the batter will not rise and become light. The non-stick spray actually prevents the cookies from getting tall and light.

Put the flour, baking soda, oats and salt in a bowl and whisk with a wire whisk until well combined and set aside. Cream the shortening, brown sugar and peanut butter in a mixer bowl beating until until creamy. Add the egg and vanilla and beat in.

Add the flour mixture gradually to the shortening mixture until all is well combined. Remove from mixer and hand mix in the peanuts.

Pour into the prepared baking dish and bake for 25 minutes or until the edges pull away from the pan and the center is firm. Cool and cut into bars.

Variations: Instead of using nuts, use chocolate chips or a combination of nuts and chips. If you use chocolate chunk the flavor is reminiscent of peanut butter blossoms with the candy kiss in the center. You can do that too. Just unwrap candy kisses and have them ready when the cookies come out of the oven. Press them in in rows up and down and crosswise to make sure each bar will have a kiss on top.

LEMON BARS

These bars are so lemony they taste like solid homemade lemonade. They have a slightly crispy crust and gooey lemon on top and remind you of lemon meringue pie without the meringue.

Ingredients:
1 cup butter
1/2 cup granulated sugar
2 cups all-purpose flour
4 eggs, beaten
1-1/2 cups more of granulated sugar
1/4 cup more of all-purpose flour
2 juiced lemons.

Directions:
HINT: Do not use lemon juice in the bottle as it makes these cookies taste artificial. Also avoid using margarine. Most types of inexpensive margarine has a

large water content, at least more than butter has. If you use margarine, your recipes may not come out because of the extra liquid.

Preheat your oven to 350 degrees F and cut a piece of bakers parchment paper the same size as the bottom of a 9 x 13 inch baking pan. Put the parchment at the bottom of the pan. This pan calls for an ungreased pan and the parchment will stop the bottom of the cookie from browning too much and from sticking to the pan.

Mix the butter that has been softened and the 1/2 cup of sugar and 2 cups of flour in a medium mixing bowl. You do not have to use the mixer. Just use a spoon or heavy whisk to mix everything up well. Press the finished dough into the bottom of the pan. Bake for 15 to 20 minutes or until the crust is firm and slightly browned.

In another bowl whisk the 4 beaten eggs, 1-1/2 cup sugar, 1/4 cup flour and the juice of 2 lemons. You can use the mixer for this if you want, but it will beat by hand easily. Pour this over the baked crust. You do not have to let it cool.

Bake for 20 more minutes. Do not over bake. Take them out and leave the pan on a cooling rack for 45 minutes to 1 hour. The bars will firm up as they cool. Once they are cool cut into about 36 bars and dust with powdered sugar. Keep left overs, if there are any, in an airtight container in the refrigerator.

Variations: Use lime juice instead of lemon and a touch of green food coloring for a different flavor and appearance. Add a 1/2 teaspoon of almond extract to lemon bars for a slightly different flavor.

GINGERY LEMON BARS

These bars have the flavor of ginger and lemon and they are a little different. You make a crust and then put a filling on top. This recipe makes 36 bars and they do not freeze very well, so eat them up quickly.

Ingredients:
1-1/2 cups all-purpose flour
1/4 teaspoon salt
1-1/2 stick (3/4 cup) softened unsalted butter
1/3 cup confectioners' sugar
1/2 teaspoon grated lemon zest
1/2 cup crystallized ginger that has been minced fine
3/4 teaspoon ground ginger
3 large eggs
6 Tablespoons fresh lemon juice
1-1/3 cups granulated sugar
3 more tablespoons flour
1/2 teaspoon baking powder

1/2 teaspoon more grated lemon zest

Directions:
Preheat the oven to 350 degrees and spray the bottom (not the sides) of a 9 by 13 inch baking pan.

Whisk the flour and salt together in a bowl and set aside. Cream the butter in a mixer and add the confectioners sugar and beat until light and smooth. Add the first 1/2 teaspoon lemon zest, crystallized ginger, ground ginger and mix well. Gradually add the flour mixture to the butter mixture until it is all incorporated. Spread in the bottom of the baking pan and bake 12 to 15 minutes or until slightly brown. Remove from the oven.

While the crust is baking, use a wire whisk to beat the eggs, lemon juice, granulated sugar, 3 more tablespoons of flour, baking powder and second 1/2 teaspoon of lemon zest. Whip well. The mixture will be runny and easy to pour evenly over the crust.

Put back in the oven for another 15 to 20 minutes or until the top turns golden. Cool on a cooling rack. Dust with a little more confecionters' sugar and cut into bars. Store in an airtight container.

BANANA BARS

These bars are almost like a banana cake with cream cheese frosting and will literally fly out of the cookie jar. They make about 36 bars so a double batch is great to take to a church or social function. You will need a 10 x 15 inch jelly roll pan to make these bars because if you make them too thick, they don't bake up right.

Ingredients:
2 cups all-purpose flour
1 teaspoon baking soda
1/4 teaspoon salt
1/2 cup softened butter
1-1/2 cups granulated sugar
2 eggs
1-1/4 cup sour cream
1 teaspoon vanilla flavoring
1 cup mashed, peeled, ripe banana
1 – 8 oz package of cream cheese, softened
1/4 cup more softened butter
1 cup confectioners' sugar
1/2 teaspoon more vanilla flavoring

Directions:

Preheat the oven to 350 degrees F and prepare a 10 x 15 inch jelly roll pan with non-stick spray.

In a large bowl place the flour, baking soda and salt and whisk with a wire whisk to combine. Set this mixture aside. Cream the butter and sugar in a mixer bowl until it becomes creamy and smooth. Beat in the 2 eggs, one at a time. Add the sour cream and the 1 teaspoon vanilla flavoring. Add the dry ingredients to the ingredients in the mixer gradually making sure each addition is mixed in well. Add the bananas and stir in by hand. Scrape the batter into the prepared jelly roll pan and spread it out evenly. Bake for 20 to 25 minutes or until a toothpick poked in the center comes out clean. Cool the bars completely and frost.

To make the frosting combine the cream cheese, 1/4 cup softened butter, confectioners' sugar and remaining vanilla and cream in the mixture until smooth. Spread on the cooled bar cookies, wait about 15 minutes for the frosting to set and cut into bars.

Variations: Add 1/2 cup chopped nuts to the bars or sprinkle the frosting with crushed nuts. Add 3/4 cup mini chocolate chips to the bars and sprinkle a few on the top. Banana and chocolate tastes very good together.

BLUEBERRY BARS

These bars will turn your teeth violet for a little bit, but it is worth it. Those that love blueberries will love these great bars made with fresh fruit. The crust is very crumbly but delicious. This recipe makes about 15 servings so if you are having a crowd, make two batches.

Ingredients:
1 cup granulated sugar
1 teaspoon baking powder
3 cups all-purpose flour
1-1/4 cup shortening
1 egg
1/4 teaspoon salt
1/8 teaspoon cinnamon
4 cups fresh blueberries
1/2 cup more granulated sugar
3 teaspoons cornstarch

Directions:
Preheat the oven to 375 degrees F and prepare a 9 x 13 baking pan on bottom and sides with non-stick spray.

In a medium sized bowl combine the 1 cup of sugar, flour and baking powder. Whisk with a wire whisk until well combined. Add in the salt and the cinnamon. Now use a pastry cutter to cut in the shortening and beaten egg. The dough will be moist and crumbly. Place half of this dough into the baking pan and press it into the bottom. Set aside the rest.

Place the blueberries, 1/2 cup sugar, and cornstarch in another medium bowl and gently toss the blueberries to coat. Be careful not to squash them or break them up too much. Pour over the crust mixture in the baking pan. Take the rest of the crust mixture and crumble it over top the blueberry mixture.

Bake for 45 minutes or until the bars are bubbly and slightly brown on the top. Cool them completely before cutting them into bars.

7 LAYER BARS

These are a popular cookie that came out in the 1960s and 1970s. They actually have 7 layers of sweet goodness. They are super easy to make. This recipe makes about 36 bars and they are hard to keep away from the family, but they are really rich too so a little goes a long way. I don't even want to know what the calorie count is of these cookies.

Ingredients:
1/2 cup unsalted butter (do not use salted butter because they will be too salty)
1-1/2 cups graham cracker crumbs (make your own by placing crackers in between 2 pieces of wax paper and running a rolling pin over top.
1 cup semi-sweet chocolate chips
1 cup butterscotch chips
1 cup chopped walnuts
1-14 ounce can sweetened condensed milk
1-1/2 cups shredded coconut (the bagged kind is ok, but fresh shredded is better).

Directions:
Preheat the oven to 350 degrees.

Place the butter in a 13 by 9 inch pan and put it in the oven for about 8 minutes or until the butter melts. Tip the pan so that the butter coats the bottom and sides of the pan. Pour in graham cracker crumbs to cover the bottom of the pan. Layer over the chocolate chips, then the butterscotch chips, then the nuts. Pour the can of milk evenly over the top. Sprinkle with the coconut. Bake about 25 minutes or until the edges are light golden brown. Let them cool before cutting into bars

Variations: There are so many things you can do with this recipe. Use peanut butter chips instead of butterscotch chips. Add dried cherries, raisins, currants or cranberries after the chips.

CRANBERRY BARS

These bars are perfect for the holidays including Thanksgiving or Christmas, but if you like cranberries you can make them anytime. They are tart and sweet at the same time.

Ingredients:
1-12 ounce package whole cranberries
1 cup granulated sugar
3/4 cup orange juice
1-18.25 ounce packages of yellow cake mix
3/4 cup butter, melted
2 eggs, beaten
1 cup rolled oats (Old Fashion, not the quick kind)
3/4 cup light brown sugar that is packed
1 teaspoon ground ginger
1 teaspoon ground cinnamon

Directions:
Put the cranberries in a saucepan over medium heat with the granulated sugar and orange juice. Stir occasionally and cook until the cranberries pop and the mixture thickens. This will take about 15 minutes. Remove the pan from the heat and set it aside to cool down.

Meanwhile, preheat your oven to 350 degrees F. Cut a piece of parchment to fit into the bottom of a 9 x 13 inch baking pan and put it in.

In a mixing bowl combine the cake mix, melted butter and beaten eggs. Beat until well combined. Add the rolled oats, brown sugar, ginger and cinnamon and beat well. Reserve 1 -1/2 cups of this mixture and spread the rest in the bottom of the prepared pan. Make the mixture as even as possible to make a crust. Pour the cranberry mixture over the crust. Make a ball with the reserved mixture and pinch off pieces to place over the cranberry mixture in the pan. Bake for 35 to 40 minutes or until the top is a light brown. Cool for 40 minutes before cutting into 24 bars.

ALMOND MERINGE RASPBERRY BARS

These are fancy cookies, but the family might like them for special occasions. Take these to a pot luck dinner and you will get raves.

Ingredients:
1 cup softened butter
7 ounces almond paste (this usually comes in a tube)
1/2 cup brown sugar packed
1 egg
1 teaspoon almond extract
2 cups all-purpose flour
3/4 cup seedless raspberry jam

3 egg whites
1/2 cup white sugar
1/2 cup flaked coconut

Directions:
Preheat the oven to 350 degrees F and line a 9 by 13 inch pan with aluminum foil, shiny side up. Spray with non-stick spray.

Make the crust in a large bowl by mixing the butter, almond paste and brown sugar until it is smooth. Beat in the egg and almond extract and add the flour gradually until well mixed. Place in the bottom of the pan pressing in tightly. Bake for 20 to 25 minutes or until the crust is golden brown. Cool for about 20 minutes and spread with raspberry jam.

In a large glass or very clean metal bowl, whip the egg whites with a mixer until they start to form soft peaks. Gradually add the 1/2 cup sugar until the peaks are stiff. Spread this meringue over the jam and sprinkle it with coconut flakes. Bake 15 to 20 minutes more or until the meringue is firm. Let the pan cool on wire racks and cut the bars with a very sharp knife.

APPLE BARS

These bars have the spicy taste of tart apples, cinnamon, nutmeg, ginger and nuts to make a delicious combination.

Ingredients:
1 cup all-purpose flour
1 teaspoon baking powder
1/8 teaspoon salt
1/4 teaspoon ground cinnamon
1/4 teaspoon ground nutmeg
1/8 teaspoon ground ginger
1/4 cup butter
1/2 cup brown sugar packed
1/2 cup granulated sugar
1 egg
1 teaspoon vanilla
3/4 cup chopped tart apple (McIntosh or Ida Red are good)
1/2 cup chopped nuts
2 tablespoons more of granulated sugar
2 teaspoons more of ground cinnamon

Directions:

Preheat the oven to 350 degrees F and spray a 9 x 9 inch pan with non stick spray.

Place the flour, baking powder, salt and first set of spices in a bowl. Set it aside. In a separate large bowl mix the melted butter, brown sugar and 1/2 cup granulated sugar. Use a wooden spoon. Beat the egg in a small bowl and add it to the mixture along with vanilla. Gradually add the flour mixture and fold in just to combine. Stir in the apples and nuts. Spread the mixture into the prepared pan.

In a small bowl mix the 2 tablespoons granulated sugar and cinnamon and sprinkle it on top. Bake for 25 to 30 minutes until the bars spring back when touched. Cool in the pan about 1 hour and cut into 16 bars.

Variations: Use peaches instead of apples.

SALTED CARAMEL PECAN BARS

These cookies come out a little between a cookie and peanut brittle. You can break them into bars and they are thin and rouged. The flavor is beyond compare and everyone will ask for more. This recipe makes about 2 to 3 dozen.

Ingredients:
1 cup chopped pecans
12 whole graham crackers
3/4 cup butter
1 cup brown sugar packed tight
2 tablespoons heavy whipping cream
1 -1/2 teaspoon vanilla
1/2 teaspoon sea salt

Directions:
Preheat your oven to 350 degrees F and place in a shallow pan to bake for 10 to 12 minutes. Stir halfway through the time. Remove from oven and set aside.

Take aluminum foil and line a 15 by 10 inch jelly roll pan spraying with non-stick spray. Make sure a large part of the foil hangs over each 10 inch rim and fold it over. You will be using this as handles to slide the cookies off the pan. Place the graham crackers on the bottom of the pan, overlapping them slightly so they fit over the entire bottom.

Place the butter and brown sugar in a heavy saucepan over medium heat and melt, stirring frequently. Let it come to a boil. Turn off the heat and add the vanilla and toasted pecans. Pour this mixture over the graham crackers evenly and bake for 10 to 11 minutes. Remove from oven and immediately sprinkle with the sea salt and and slide the foil out of the pan and onto a cooling rack carefully. Cool about 30 minutes and break into bars.

Variation: After baking and removing from the oven, sprinkle over 1 cup of semi-sweet chocolate chips. Wait about 2 to 3 minutes and spread over top of the bars and let cool to harden before breaking into bars.

RICE CEREAL BARS WITH A COUPLE TWISTS

Everyone should know how to make rice cereal treats with marshmallow cream. This recipe makes bars with a twist.

Ingredients:
5 cups chocolate rice cereal
1/4 cup butter
1-7 oz jar marshmallow cream
1/4 teaspoon peppermint extract
1 cup candy coated chocolate candy

Directions:
Place the butter in a medium sauce pan and melt. Add the marshmallow cream and cook over low making sure to stir constantly with a wooden spoon until cream and butter are all melted and blended. Remove from the heat and add the peppermint extract.

Place the rice cereal in a large bowl. Pour the butter mixture over top and mix well. Let the mixture cool slightly and add the candy coated chocolate candy and mix well. Use your hands if you like. Pack the mixture into a buttered 9 by 13 inch pan and let cool completely. Cut into 24 squares.

Variations: Use chocolate chips or fruit flavored candy coated candy instead. Omit the peppermint extract and try almond extract. You can also add chopped nuts to this recipe with great results.

Chapter 3: Mouth Watering Drop Cookies

The name drop cookies implies that you drop them, and you do. Drop cookies are made by taking a portion of the dough and dropping it on a cookie sheet. Sometimes you use spoons to scoop it out and put it on the cookie sheet and sometimes you just grab a hunk of dough, roll it and put it on the cookie sheet. Some drop cookies are flattened using a fork or the bottom of a glass. The most popular drop cookie is the Toll House or Chocolate Chip cookie.

CHOCOLATE CHIP COOKIES

My recipe is a little different from the original. I use a few different measurements and I use shortening instead of butter. The shortening makes the cookie a little crispier on the outside, but the inside is very soft and gooey.

Ingredients:
2-1/4 cups all-purpose flour
1 teaspoon baking soda
1/2 teaspoon salt
1 cup shortening
3/4 cup granulated sugar
3/4 cup brown sugar, packed tightly
1-1/2 teaspoons vanilla
2 large eggs
1-12 oz package of chocolate chips

Directions:
Preheat the oven to 375 degrees F and cover several baking sheets with parchment paper.

Combine the flour, baking soda, and salt in a large bowl and whisk to combine it all together. Put the shortening, granulated and brown sugar in a mixer bowl and beat on high until it becomes creamy. Add the vanilla and the eggs and mix in well.

Add the flour mixture gradually beating it totally in before adding the next spoonful. Continue until all the flour mixture is mixed in. This batter will be stiff. Remove from the mixer and hand mix in the chocolate chips using a large wooden spoon.

Drop the batter by teaspoonfuls onto the parchment paper. Space the cookies about 1-1/2 inches apart. You can usually put 4 across and 5 down on a standard large cookie sheet. Bake for 9 to 12 minutes or until the cookies are a light brown. Set the cookie sheet on a cooling rack and cool for 2 minutes before removing the cookies to the cooling rack.

This recipe makes about 5 dozen. These cookies freeze very well and will stay fresh for a few months in the freezer. You can also freeze this cookie dough in increments and take them out to thaw. Once thawed put the dough on the cookie sheets and bake.

Variations: Use Candy Coated Chocolate candy instead of the chocolate chips. You can add 1 cup chopped nuts or only use the nuts. Use 3/4 cup chopped macadamia nuts and 3/4 cup vanilla chips for another variation.

OATMEAL RAISIN COOKIE

This is another old favorite my grandmother made. The cookies are light and crispy outside with gooey raisins mixed in. Again, I use shortening because it makes the cookie a little more crispy, but you can use butter instead for a little more dense cookie.

Ingredients:
1 -1/4 cup all-purpose flour
1 teaspoon baking soda
1/2 teaspoon salt
2-3/4 cups rolled oats
3/4 cup shortening
3/4 cup granulated sugar
3/4 cup light brown sugar, packed tight
2 large eggs
1 teaspoon vanilla
1 cup raisins

Directions:
Preheat your oven to 375 degrees F and cover several cookie sheets with parchment paper.

Whisk together the flour, baking soda, salt and rolled oats in a large bowl and set aside. With a mixer, cream the shortening, granulated and brown sugar until it is creamy and smooth. Add the eggs and vanilla and beat until the mixture is fluffy.

Gradually add the flour mixture to the shortening mixture beating well after every addition. The batter will become very stiff and thick. Mix in the raisins by hand using a wooden spoon and a some muscle.

Drop by teaspoonful's onto the parchment covered cookie sheets spacing about 1-1/2 inch apart. (4 across and 5 down on a large sheet) Bake for 8 to 10 minutes or until golden. Cool for about 2 minutes on the cookie sheet and remove cookies to the cooling rack.

This makes about 3 dozen cookies. These cookies also freeze well after being baked.

Variations: Instead of raisins add 1/2 cup dried cranberries and 1/2 cup slivered almonds. You can also add chopped nuts to the original recipe.

PEANUT BUTTER COOKIES

Who doesn't like peanut butter cookies? These are the kind that your grandmother probably made with the cross hatch of a fork imprinted on the top. They are crispy on the outside and light on the inside with that distinctive peanut butter flavor.

Ingredients:
3-1/2 cups all-purpose flour
1-1/2 teaspoon baking soda
1 teaspoon salt
1 cup shortening
2-1/2 cups light brown sugar packed tight
1-1/2 cup smooth peanut butter
2 eggs
3/8 cup milk (if you don't have a 3/8 measuring cup use 6 tablespoons)
2 tablespoons vanilla

Directions:
Preheat oven to 375 degrees and cover several cookie sheets with parchment paper.

Whisk together the flour, baking soda and salt in a large bowl until it is well combined and set aside. Cream shortening and brown sugar in a mixing bowl until it is light and creamy. Add the peanut butter and cream in well.

In a small bowl, combine the eggs, milk and vanilla. Mix this into the shortening mixture until it is well combined. Add the flour mixture gradually to the mixture in the mixer until it is well combined. The dough will be thick.

Drop by teaspoonful's onto the parchment covered baking sheets leaving about 1-1/2 inch around each cookie (4 across and 5 down). Press lightly on the top of each cookie with a fork one way and the across the other way. Do not press hard. You don't want to flatten the cookie too much or it won't rise and cook correctly to make a light cookie. Bake for 8 to 10 minutes and remove and let cool 2 minutes before removing cookies to a cooling rack.

This will make about 5 to 6 dozen cookies. These cookies freeze well after being baked and will last a few months in the freezer.

Variations: Add 1 cup chopped peanuts to the batter before baking, or you can sprinkle some chopped peanuts on top of each cookie before depressing with a fork. Another variation is to add one 12 oz package of chocolate chips so your cookies will taste something like a peanut butter cup.

GINGER SNAPS

These spicy cookies are some of my favorites. They are often called molasses cookies too because of the addition of molasses to the batter. Roll them in pastel colored sugar before baking and they will come out glittery.

Ingredients:
4 cups all-purpose flour
1-1/2 teaspoons ground ginger
1-1/2 teaspoons ground cinnamon
1-1/2 teaspoons ground allspice
3-1/2 teaspoons baking soda
1 teaspoon salt
2-1/2 cups shortening
3-1/2 cups granulated sugar
2/4 cup molasses
2 eggs
1 teaspoon vanilla

Directions:
Preheat the oven to 350 degrees and line several baking sheets with parchment paper.

Whisk together the flour, spices, baking soda and salt until well combined. Set this mixture aside. In the mixer cream the shortening, sugar and molasses until light and creamy. Add the eggs and vanilla and mix in well. Gradually the dry ingredients to the wet mixture until it is well combined.

Scoop out teaspoonful's of the dough and roll into a ball by hand. Place in a bowl of colored sugar and coat all sides. Place on the parchment covered baking sheets (4 across and 5 down on large sheet) evenly spaced. Press down lightly with two fingers to flatten a little.

Bake 9 minutes and remove from oven to cool on baking sheet about 2 minutes. Remove to cooling racks until completely cool.

This recipe makes 3 dozen cookies which will freeze well after being baked.

PECAN SANDY COOKIES

These cookies are full of pecans and they have a shortbread, sandy type texture. They don't taste like sand though. They are sweet and crunchy with the flavor of pecans. This recipe makes 2 dozen cookies

Ingredients:
2 cups all-purpose flour
1/4 teaspoon salt
1 cup softened unsalted butter
1/2 cup granulated sugar
1/2 cup confectioners' sugar
1 teaspoon vanilla
1 cup chopped pecans

Directions:
Preheat your oven to 350 degrees F and cover cookie sheets with parchment paper.

Whisk the flour and salt together in a bowl and set aside. Place the butter and granulated sugar in a mixer bowl and cream together until smooth. Slowly add the confectioners' sugar until mixed in. Add the vanilla and beat. Gradually add the flour mixture to the butter mixture creating a soft dough. Hand stir the pecans into the dough.

Scoop out the dough by teaspoonfuls and roll them into balls placing them 1 inch apart on the covered cookie sheets. Bake about 18 to 20 minutes or until the edges turn golden. Cool on baking sheets for about 5 minutes and remove to cooling racks.

SNICKERDOODLES

This cinnamon flavored cookie has an interesting name that doesn't really have an origin. It has a crackled top and delightful spicy flavor.
Ingredients:
3-3/4 cups all-purpose flour
1/2 teaspoon baking soda
1/2 teaspoon cream of tartar
1/4 teaspoon salt
1 cup shortening
2 cups granulated sugar
2 large eggs
1/4 cup milk
1 tablespoon vanilla
1 teaspoon almond extract
3 more tablespoons granulated sugar
1 more teaspoon ground cinnamon
2 teaspoons brown sugar

Directions:
Whisk together the flour, baking soda, cream of tartar and the salt until well combined. Set aside

Cream the shortening and 2 cups of granulated sugar in the mixer until it is creamy and smooth. Stir in the eggs, vanilla and almond extract and mix well. Gradually mix in the flour mixture until it is all well combined. Cover the bowl with plastic wrap and refrigerate for about 2 hours.

When the 2 hours is almost up, preheat your oven to 375 degrees and prepare baking pans by covering with parchment paper.

In a small bowl whisk together the 3 tablespoons granulated sugar, 1 teaspoon cinnamon and 2 teaspoons brown sugar. Mix it thoroughly. Scoop out teaspoonful's of dough and roll into 1 inch balls by hand. Roll the balls in the sugar cinnamon mixture and place on cookie sheets about 2 inches apart.

Bake about 8 minutes or until the top starts to crack and edges brown. Remove immediately to cooling racks and cool.

This makes approximately 2 dozen cookies. These don't freeze very well as they tend to get a little soggy when defrosted.

ALMOND COOKIES

These cookies are made with a little bit of amaretto and they are really delicious. The recipe only makes about 2 dozen, but these cookies do not freeze well and have to be eaten up within a few days. They may or may not last that long.

Ingredients:
1-1/4 cups all-purpose flour
1/2 cup ground almonds
1/8 teaspoon salt
1/2 cup shortening (butter makes a more dense cookie)
1/2 cup granulated sugar
1 egg
2 teaspoons almond flavoring
2 teaspoons amaretto

Directions:
Preheat oven to 400 degrees F and cover several cookie sheets with parchment paper.

Whisk together in a large bowl the flour, ground almonds and salt until well combined and set aside. Cream the shortening and sugar in a mixer until light. Beat in the egg, almond flavoring and amaretto until light and creamy.

Gradually add the dry ingredients to the shortening mixture until it is all mixed in well.

Drop dough by teaspoonfuls onto the parchment paper about 2 inches apart. Bake 5 to 9 minutes or until the cookies become light brown on the edges. Cool on cookie sheet 2 minutes before removing them to cooling racks.

Variation: Top each cookie with a sliver of maraschino cherry before popping it into the oven. You can also top each cookie with a slivered almond right after removing from the oven. Just lightly press it into the cookie.

DROP SUGAR COOKIES

Old fashion vanilla flavored drop sugar cookies are the best. This recipe comes from way back and uses buttermilk to give the cookies a richness that cannot be compared.

Ingredients:
2 cups all-purpose flour
1/2 teaspoon baking powder
1/4 teaspoon salt
1 cup shortening
2 cups granulated sugar
2 eggs
1-1/2 cup buttermilk
1 teaspoon vanilla
1/2 to 3/4 cup more of granulated sugar

Directions:
Whisk the flour, baking soda and salt in a medium bowl until well combined. Set this mixture aside. In the mixer, cream the shortening and white sugar until creamy. Add the egg, buttermilk and vanilla and beat until light. Gradually add the flour mixture to the shortening mixture combining well between each addition. Cover the mixing bowl with plastic wrap and chill in the refrigerator for about an hour.

About 15 minutes before the hour is up, preheat the oven to 400 degrees and cover several cookie sheets with parchment paper. Remove dough from refrigerator and scoop out teaspoonfuls and roll into 1 inch balls by hand. Roll the balls in the 1/2 to 3/4 cup granulated sugar in a shallow bowl before placing about 2 inches apart on baking sheets.

Bake cookies for about 7 to 9 minutes or until they turn a light brown around the edges. Cool on cookie sheets for about 2 minutes before transferring to cooling racks.

Variation: Use colored sugar to roll the cookies in to make them look more festive.

FROSTED PUMPKIN DROP COOKIES

These are a favorite around Halloween and Thanksgiving, but they use canned pumpkin, so they can be made all year round. If you like pumpkin pie, you will love these cookies. The frosting makes them all the sweeter. They are a very soft cookie that mounds up. This recipe makes 3 dozen cookies and they can be frozen after baking, but often are a little soggy when they thaw. It is best to eat them right away, within a few days.

Ingredients:
2-1/2 cups all-purpose flour
1 teaspoon baking powder
1 teaspoon baking soda
2 teaspoons ground cinnamon
1/2 teaspoon ground nutmeg
1/4 teaspoon ground cloves
1/4 teaspoon ground ginger
1/4 teaspoon salt
1/2 cup softened buttermilk
1-1-2 cup granulated sugar
1 cup pureed pumpkin in a can
1 large egg
1-1/2 teaspoon vanilla
2 cups confectioners' sugar
3 tablespoons milk
1 tablespoon melted buttermilk
1 teaspoon more vanilla

Directions:
Preheat your oven to 350 degrees F and prepare several baking sheets by covering them with parchment paper.

Whisk together the flour, baking powder, baking soda, spices and salt in a large bowl until well combined.

In the mixer beat the 1/2 cup softened butter, granulated sugar and pumpkin until creamy. Add the egg and 1 teaspoon vanilla and beat in well. Add the dry ingredients to the mixture in the mixer gradually mixing in well every time you add until all is incorporated.

Drop onto the cookie sheet about 2 inches apart (4 across and 5 down)and flatten slightly with your fingers. Bake for about 15 to 20 minutes and remove to cool on racks for about 2 minutes. Remove the cookies to the racks and let them cool completely.

Mix the frosting glaze in a small bowl by whisking the confectioners sugar, milk, 1 teaspoon melted butter and 1 teaspoon vanilla. Add more milk as needed to make it so the mixture can be drizzled over top. Start at the center and make circles out to the edges making sure to cover completely. Some of the glaze will drip off the cookies so make sure to place a piece of newspaper under the cooling racks for easy clean up.

Variation: Add 2 tablespoons cocoa powder to the frosting glaze and/or add 3/4 cup chocolate chips, beaten in by hand.

TROPICAL COCONUT DROPS

If you love the flavor of coconut, you will love these cookies. They are cake-like with flaked coconut mixed in. They give you a little taste of the tropics in a chewy cookie that makes about 3 dozen. These do not freeze well so eat them up quickly.

Ingredients:
1-1/4 cups all-purpose flour
1/2 teaspoon baking soda
1/4 teaspoon salt
1/2 cup butter
1/2 cup brown sugar packed tight
1/2 cup granulated sugar
1 egg
1 teaspoon vanilla
1-1/2 cups flaked coconut

Directions:
Preheat your oven to 350 degrees and prepare several baking sheets by covering them with parchment paper.

Whisk together the flour, baking soda and salt in a large bowl until it is well combined. Set this bowl aside.

In your mixer cream the butter, brown sugar and granulated sugar until smooth. Beat in the egg and vanilla until the mixture becomes fluffy. Gradually add the flour mixture to the butter mixture beating in well after every addition. Mix in the coconut by hand.

Drop by teaspoonfuls onto the prepared baking sheets. These spread so you need to space wide at 3 inches apart (3 across and 4 down). Bake 8 to 10 minutes or until the coconut looks toasted and the cookies are firm. Cool on the pan 2 minutes before removing to cooling sheets.

Variations: This recipe is a little delicate and adding anything might throw it off. You can however use food coloring to color the coconut before adding it to give it a festive color.

Apple Cookies

These cookies are spicy and moist like cake. There are many ingredients, but it is worth it when you take a bite and taste the apples and spices in a rich cookie. This recipe only makes 18 cookies, but you don't want to make many since they do not keep well. They also get soggy when frozen.

Ingredients:
2 cups all-purpose flour
1 teaspoon baking soda
1/4 teaspoon salt
1 teaspoon ground cinnamon
1/4 teaspoon ground cloves
1/4 teaspoon ground ginger
1/4 teaspoon ground nutmeg
1/2 cup shortening
1-1/2 cup brown sugar packed
1 egg
1/2 teaspoon vanilla
1 cup peeled, cored and diced apples (use a good baking apple like MacIntosh)
1 cup raisins
1/4 cup milk
1-1/2 cups confectioners' sugar
1 tablespoon butter that has been melted
1/2 teaspoon more of vanilla
2-1/2 tablespoons half and half (cream)

Directions:
Preheat your oven to 400 degrees F and prepare 2 cookie sheets by covering them with parchment paper and spraying with non stick spray.

Whisk together the flour, baking soda, salt and spices until well combined and set aside. Cream the shortening and the brown sugar together until it becomes creamy and smooth. Add the egg and vanilla and beat in well. Gradually add the flour mixture to the combination in the mixer mixer mixing well after each addition. The batter will be very thick. Add the milk and hand stir in the apples and raisins.

Drop by tablespoonfuls onto the prepared cookie sheet about 1-1/2 inches apart (4 across 5 down) and bake 10 to 12 minutes until lightly brown and firm. Remove from the pan to wire racks while still warm.

In a small bowl whisk the confectioners' sugar, melted butter, vanilla and the milk until it is creamy and can be spread. Spread on the warm cookies at let cool.

Variation: Add 1 cup chopped walnuts or any type of nut to the mix when mixing in the raisins and apples.

BROWN BUTTER COOKIES

This is an old recipe with a delicious flavor. It is a cake like cookie with a glaze and tastes a little like butterscotch. This recipe makes about 3 dozen cookies. They do not freeze well so make sure you can eat them up in a few days.

Ingredients:
1 cup butter (do not use margarine or shortening)
1 cup brown sugar packed tight
1 egg
1-1/4 teaspoon vanilla
1/2 teaspoon baking soda
1/4 teaspoon baking powder
1/4 teaspoon salt
1-1/2 cups all-purpose flour
2/3 cup pecans chopped
1 teaspoon more vanilla
1-3/4 cup confectioners' sugar (you may not use this much)
1/4 cup hot water

Directions:
Preheat oven to 350 degrees and prepare several baking sheets by covering them with parchment paper.

Heat butter in a saucepan over medium heat for about 3 to 5 minutes or until it turns a little bit brown. It will foam and bubble, but do not let it burn. Remove from heat and cool. Take out 1/4 cup of the browned butter and save for the frosting.

Pour remaining browned butter into a mixer bowl and add the brown sugar. Beat until creamy the butter is cool. Add the egg. (Be careful here. If the butter is still hot it will cook the egg and make your cookies lumpy with what looks like scrambled egg in them. If the mixture is cool, you don't have to worry.) Add the vanilla and beat in well.

In a different bow combine the baking soda, baking powder, salt and flour. Whisk it together well. Gradually mix in the flour mixture. Mix in the pecans by hand and drop onto prepared baking sheets about 1-1/2 inches apart.

Bake for about 10 minutes or until the cookie turns a light brown on the edges. Cool on pans for 2 minutes and remove to cooling racks.

Prepare frosting by mixing the reserved brown butter with the 1 teaspoon vanilla, hot water and confectioners' sugar. Add enough to make a semi thick icing. Beat until smooth and slater on to the tops of the cookies. Let the frosting cool and set.

Variation: Use walnuts or even peanuts for a different flavor.

MAPLE SYRUP COOKIES

These cookies really bring the season of fall to the table. They are made with real maple syrup. Don't try to substitute any of the maple flavored syrup, it has to be the stuff that comes directly from the trees and is boiled down to a sugary, sticky sweetness. This recipe only about 18 cookies and are one of those things that should be a seasonal "only once in awhile" treat. Real maple syrup isn't cheap!

Ingredients
1-1/2 cups all-purpose flour
2 teaspoons baking powder
1/4 teaspoon salt
1/2 cup shortening
1 cup brown sugar that is packed tight
1 egg
1/2 cup maple syrup
1 teaspoon vanilla
1 cup coconut that is flaked

Directions:
Preheat your oven to 375 degrees F and prepare at cookies sheet by cutting parchment paper to fit on top. Spray non-stick spray on the parchment paper.

Whisk together the flour, baking powder and salt in another bowl until well combined and set aside. In your mixer bowl, cream the shortening and brown sugar. Add the egg and beat in until creamy. Add the maple syrup and vanilla and beat until smooth. Add the dry ingredients to the ingredients in the mixer gradually until it is all well combined. Remove the bowl from the mixer and fold the coconut in by hand.

Drop by tablespoonfuls onto the cookies sheet leaving 2 inches between each cookie. These really spread so only do 3 across and 4 down on a large cookie sheet. Bake for about 10-12 minutes or until brown and set. Let sit on cookie sheet about 2 minutes before removing to cooling racks.

Variations: Instead of coconut, add 3/4 cup toasted pecans or other nuts.

BANANA COOKIES

These cookies are much like banana nut bread and they are really good. You can make them without the frosting, but they taste so much better with it. This recipe makes about 18 large cookies that the family will love. They do not stay fresh long, so it is better to make small batches more frequently than let them go to waste because they become stale. This recipe uses both shortening and butter. The addition of the butter makes the cookie more cake-like and also makes it very rich.

Ingredients:
1/2 cup shortening
1/2 cup softened butter
1 cup granulated sugar
2 eggs
1 cup mashed banana
1/2 cup evaporated milk – save the rest for the frosting
1-1/4 teaspoon vanilla
1 teaspoon white vinegar
3 cups all-purpose flour
1 teaspoon baking soda
1/4 teaspoon salt
1 cup chopped walnuts
2-1/2 cups confectioners' sugar
2 tablespoons more softened butter
1/4 cup more evaporated milk
1/2 teaspoon more vanilla

Directions:
place the shortening, 1/2 cup butter, granulated sugar in a mixer bowl and mix until creamy and smooth. Add the eggs, bananas, vanilla, 1/2 cup evaporated milk and vinegar until everything is smooth and creamy.

Whisk together the flour, baking soda and salt in another bowl. Add this mixture to the shortening/butter mixture gradually mixing well after every addition. Hand mix the walnuts in. Cover the bowl with plastic wrap and place in the refrigerator for about 1 hour or overnight.

Preheat the oven to 375 degrees and cover baking sheets with parchment paper spraying with a little non-stick spray.

Drop the dough by teaspoonfuls onto the cookie sheet 2 inches apart (3 across and 4 down). Bake about 15 minutes and remove to cooling racks to cool completely before frosting.

To make the frosting combine the confectioners' sugar, 2 tablespoons butter, 1/4 cup evaporated milk and 1/4 teaspoon vanilla in the mixer bowl beating until soft and smooth. Spread on the tops of the cooled cookies.

Variations: You can use just about any nut with this cookie. If you don't like walnuts, try pecans. You can also substitute the nuts for raisins or chocolate chips.

ORANGE POPPY SEED DROP COOKIES

This easy recipe makes a good 3-1/2 dozen cookies that are orangy and have a little crunch from the poppy seeds. They kind of taste like orange poppy seed muffins with their cake-like consistency.

Ingredients:
1-1/4 cup flour
1/2 teaspoon baking soda
pinch of salt
1/2 cup softened butter
2/3 cup granulated sugar
1 egg that has been brought to room temperature
1 tablespoon orange zest
1 teaspoon vanilla or orange extract
1 tablespoon poppy seeds

Directions:
About 1 hour before starting to bake, take the egg out of the refrigerator, place it in a bowl and let it come to room temperature.

Preheat your oven to 350 degrees F and cover cookie sheets with parchment paper.

Whisk the flour, baking soda and salt in a medium bowl until combined. Set aside. Cream the butter in the mixer and add the sugar beating until smooth and fluffy. Add the egg, orange zest and vanilla or orange extract and beat until mixed in well. Gradually add the flour mixture to the butter mixture. Fold the poppy seeds in by hand.

Drop by rounded teaspoonfuls onto a baking sheet 2 inches apart and bake for 10 to 12 minutes or until golden on edges. Set cookie sheets to cool for 5 minutes and transfer cookies to cooling racks.

Lemon Cooler Cookies

There used to be a company that made these lemon cookies dipped in confectioners' sugar and they actually made you feel cooler when you ate them. I haven't been able to find them for years and these cookies taste very much like them and sometimes even better.

Ingredients:
3 cups all-purpose flour

1/4 teaspoon salt
1 tablespoon lemon zest
1 cup softened unsalted butter
1 cup confectioners sugar
2 tablespoon fresh lemon juice
1/3 cup more confectioners' sugar
1-1/2 teaspoon more lemon zest

Preheat the oven to 325 degrees F and cover cookie sheets with parchment paper.

Whisk together the flour, salt and 1 tablespoon lemon zest in a medium bowl and set aside. Place the butter in the mixer and cream. Add confectioners' sugar and beat until soft and fluffy. Add in the lemon juice. Gradually add the flour mixture to the butter mixture until it is all incorporated.

Scoop by teaspoonful's and place on prepared cookie sheets about 1 inch apart. Flatten the balls with your fingers and shape into crescents or moons. Bake for 15 to 20 minutes or until light brown. Cool on the cookie sheet 10 minutes and continue cooling cookies on the rack. In a small bowl, combine the 1/3 cup confectioners' sugar and the 1-1/2 teaspoon lemon zest. Roll the cookies in this mixture and place back on racks to sit for about an hour. Store in an airtight container.

CHOCOLATE THUMB PRINTS

Most people know about the jam thumb prints that are popular around Christmas time (a recipe is in the Special Occasion section), but these are made with chocolate instead of jam.

Ingredients:
1 – 1/4 cups all-purpose flour
1/4 teaspoon salt
8 tablespoons (1 stick or 1/2 cup) softened unsalted butter
1/2 cup confectioners' sugar
1 teaspoon vanilla
2 ounces semi-sweet chocolate that has been finely chopped
2 tablespoons more softened unsalted butter
1/4 teaspoon corn syrup

Directions:
Preheat your oven to 350 degrees and cover cookie sheets with parchment paper.

Whisk the flour and salt in a medium bowl and set aside. Cream the 8 tablespoons butter and confectioners' sugar until light and fluffy. Add the vanilla and mix in well. Gradually add the flour mixture to the butter mixture until all mixed in.

Scoop out dough by rounded teaspoonful's and roll into a ball. Place 1 inch apart on the cookie sheets. Bake for 10 minutes and remove from the oven. Make a thumb print in the middle of the cookie but be careful to just put an indentation in and not go all the way through to the cookie sheet. You can use the back of a baby spoon if the cookies are too hot. Bake the cookies for 7 to 9 more minutes and transfer to a cooling rack to cool

When they have cooled, place the semi-sweet chocolate, 2 tablespoons butter and corn syrup in a microwave safe bowl. Cook at 50 percent in 30 second intervals stirring each time until the mixture is smooth. Let cool slightly and spoon into the indentations of the cookies. Let the chocolate cool and store in airtight containers.

CHOCOLATE ZUCCHINI COOKIES

Here is a way to get the kids to eat vegetables by making cookies with them. The zucchini has no flavor and it adds consistency to the batter and a moistness to the finished cookie. These recipe makes about 4 dozen chocolate cake-like cookies.

Ingredients:
1 -3/4 cup grated zucchini
2-1/4 cups all-purpose flour
1/3 cup unsweetened cocoa powder
1 teaspoon baking soda
1/4 teaspoon salt
1/2 cup granulated sugar
1/2 cup brown sugar packed tight
1/2 cup softened butter or shortening
1 egg
1 teaspoon vanilla

Directions:
Preheat the oven to 350 degrees F and cover with parchment paper spraying it lightly with non-stick spray.

Grate the zucchini by hand or in your food processor and place in a drainer for about 10 minutes. Squeeze between paper towels to extract as much moisture as you can.

Place the flour, cocoa powder, baking soda and salt in a bowl and whisk so that it is well combined. Set aside. Place both sugars in a mixer bowl with the butter or shortening and cream well. Add the egg and vanilla and beat that into the mixture. Gradually start adding the flour mixture by tablespoonfuls until it is all blended in. Squeeze the zucchini between paper towels one more time before adding tot he dough and folding it in.

Scoop the batter out by rounded teaspoons and place 1 inch apart on the cookie sheets. Bake 8 to 10 minutes and cool on the cookie sheet for 5 minutes before removing to a cooling rack.

ROOTIN' TOOTIN' ROOT BEER FLOAT COOKIES

Everyone loves the taste of root beer and these cookies have it. It even has a root beer flavored glaze on top for extra punch. These cookies do not freeze well and will go stale in a short time so the recipe only makes about 18 cookies.

Ingredients:
1-3/4 cups all-purpose flour
1/2 teaspoon baking soda
1/4 teaspoon salt
1 cup brown sugar packed tight
1/2 cup buttermilk1 egg
1/4 cup buttermilk
1-1/4 teaspoon root beer extract
2 cups confectioners' sugar
1/3 cup more of butter
1-1/2 teaspoons root beer extract
2 tablespoons hot water (just hot from the tap)

Directions:
Preheat your oven to 350 degrees and cover cookie sheets with parchment paper. Spray the parchment paper with non-stick spray.

Whisk together the flour baking soda and salt in a medium bowl and set aside. Use a mixing bowl and mixer to cream the brown sugar, 1/2 cup butter, egg, buttermilk and 1-1/4 teaspoon root beer extract. Add the dry ingredients gradually by tablespoonful to the butter mixture mixing in well after each addition.

Drop by teaspoonfuls 2 inches apart (3 across and 4 down) on parchment covered cookie sheets. Bake for 6 to 8 minutes or until the edges brown. Cool on racks for about 2 minutes before removing the individual cookies to the racks. Cool completely before glazing.

To make glaze mix the confectioner's sugar 1/3 cup butter and 1-1/2 teaspoons of extract with the hot water. Brush it on the top of each cookie and let it soak in for a few minutes.

Variations: You can also make these into orange cookies by using orange extract or lemon cookies by using lemon flavoring.

CRANBERRY ORANGE COOKIES

These are a regular menu item for Thanksgiving along with the pies. They have that tart but sweet flavor that makes the corners of your mouth come alive. This recipe makes about 4 dozen of the delicious cookies so you will have enough for all your guests.

Ingredients:
2-1/2 cups all-purpose flour
1/2 teaspoon baking soda
1/4 teaspoon salt
1 cup softened butter
1 cup granulated sugar
1/2 cup brown sugar packed tight
1 egg
1-1/2 teaspoon grated orange zest
2 tablespoons orange juice
2 cups chopped fresh cranberries
1/2 teaspoon more grated orange zest
3 tablespoons more orange juice
1-1/2 cup confectioners' sugar

Directions:
Preheat your oven to 375 degrees and cover cookie sheets with parchment paper.

Whisk together the flour, baking soda and salt in a medium bowl and set it aside. In your mixer bowl cream the butter, granulated sugar and brown sugar until it becomes smooth. Add the egg and beat until it is blended in. Add the 1-1/2 teaspoons orange zest and 2 tablespoons orange juice and mix in well. Add the dry ingredients gradually to the butter mixture mixing in well after each addition. Remove from the mixer and stir in the cranberries by hand until well combined.

Drop by tablespoonful's onto the cookie sheets about 2 inches apart (3 across and 4 down) and bake for about 12/14 minutes until the edges turn golden. Remove immediately to cooling racks to cool completely.

Mix the 1/2 teaspoon orange zest, 3 tablespoons orange juice and the confectioner's sugar in a small bowl until it is smooth and creamy. Spread on the top of the cookies and resist eating until the frosting is set.

Variations: Add about 1/2 cup walnuts or other nuts to the cookie with the cranberries.

LEMON CAKE MIX COOKIES

With this recipe, you can make thousands of different variations all on your own. You use a cake mix and the basics are always the same. You change the flavor of the cake mix, the flavor of the extract and the added ingredients to enhance the flavor. This recipe makes 3 dozen cake-like cookies that are good anyway you want to make them.

Ingredients:
1 package lemon cake mix
2 eggs
1/3 cup vegetable oil
1 teaspoon lemon extract
1/2 teaspoon lemon zest
1/2 cup confectioner's
1/2 teaspoon more lemon extract
1 teaspoon lemon juice

Directions:
Preheat your oven to 375 degrees F and cover several cookie sheets with parchment paper.

Pour the cake mix into the bowl of your mixer and carefully stir in the eggs, oil and lemon extract. Drop by teaspoonful's onto the cookie sheet about 1-1/2 inch apart (4 across and 5 down) and bake for 6 to 9 minutes or until edges are brown. The inside should be a bit chewy. Cook a little longer for a cake-like cookie.

Cool on cookie sheets about 2 minutes before removing to cooling racks. Cool completely before frosting.

To make frosting mix the 1/2 cup confesioners' sugar with the zest and lemon juice. If it is too thick, add a little more juice. Frost or drizzle over the cookie and let set for about 15 minutes.

Variations: There are so many. Use yellow cake mix and vanilla extract and add 1 cup chocolate chips. Use chocolate cake mix and vanilla extract and add 1 cup chopped nuts. Use strawberry cake mix and vanilla extract and add nuts and frost with chocolate glaze. This cookie has endless possibilities.

LACEY FLORENTINE COOKIES

Lace cookies, or Florentines, are a pretty cookie that look like lace. They are crunchy almost like an almond brittle with a sweet flavor. This recipe makes 3-1/2 dozen of the lace cookies.

Ingredients:
1/2 cup granulated sugar
1 cup slivered, blanched almonds
4 tablespoons softened unsalted butter-chocolate
2 tablespoons heavy cream
2 tablespoons light corn syrup
2 teaspoons vanilla

1/8 teaspoon salt
2 tablespoons light corn syrup
2 tablespoons heavy cream
1/4 teaspoon pure vanilla extract
1/8 teaspoon kosher salt
2 teaspoons all-purpose flour
4 ounces bittersweet chocolate that has been melted and is room temperature

Directions:
Process the sugar and almonds in a food processor until ground fine. Place this mixture in a heavy saucepan with the butter, corn syrup, cream, vanilla and the salt. Constantly stir over medium heat until the butter melts and the sugar has totally dissolved. This might take about 4 minutes. Remove from the burner and stir in the flour. Place in a bowl covered with plastic wrap and refrigerate until the dough is very firm, about 1 hour.

Preheat the oven to 350 degrees F and cover cookie sheets with parchment paper. Scoop out the dough by teaspoonful and roll into balls placing them 3 inches apart on the cookie sheets. Dampen your fingertips and press down until you flatten the balls to 1/4 inch thick. Bake only one sheet at a time in the preheated oven 7 to 9 minutes. Cool for 2 minutes and transfer the lacy cookies to wire racks to cool.

After the cookies are cool, melt the chocolate and spread the underside of the cookie placing it chocolate side down on parchment or wax paper lined cookie sheets. Refrigerate until the chocolate sets (about 10 minutes) Store in airtight containers.

Chapter 4: Rolled Cookies Everyone Will Love

Rolled cookies are those where the dough is rolled out flat and one of two things happen after. The cookies are cut out with cookie cutters, or a filling is spread on the flat dough and it is rolled then cut into slices and baked. Both types require a rolling pin and there are many different types out there. My personal favorite is a wooden rolling pin. When you rub flour on a wood pin, the dough usually does not stick. There are also metal rolling pins and if they are kept cold, the dough does not stick. Plastic rolling pins are usually filled with water to give them some weight. Stone rolling pins (usually marble) are very heavy and can roll dough very thing. If you don't have a rolling pin, you can also wash off a couple of soda cans and use them when they are full. Just don't open them until they rest for awhile so they do not explode.

ROLLED SUGAR AND CREAM CHEESE COOKIES

These sugar cookies are very moist and have a rich flavor of cream cheese. Make sure to soften the cream cheese and butter before you start to make them. This recipe makes quite a few cookies (about 6 to 6 1/2 doz) and they won't last long because they are so delicious.

Ingredients:
1 cup of granulated sugar
1 cup of softened butter
1 - 3 ounce package of cream cheese softened
1/4 teaspoon salt
1/2 teaspoon almond extract
1/2 teaspoon vanilla or omit the almond and add 1 teaspoon vanilla
1 egg yolk
2-1/4 cups flour

Directions:
Cream the sugar, butter, cream cheese, salt and extracts in a mixer bowl until creamy and smooth. Add the egg yolk and beet well. Add the flour gradually at 1/2 cup at a time and blend in well after each addition. Place plastic wrap over the bowl and put in the refrigerator over night or for at least 8 hours.

Preheat your oven to 375 degrees F and prepare several cookie sheets with parchment paper.

Separate the dough into 3 equal amounts. Take one handful of dough and place it on a hard floured surface. Put the other two back in the refrigerator. Roll the dough out to about 1/8 inch thick. Use a cookie cutter dipped in flour to cut out shapes. Place the shapes on a cookie sheet at least 1 inch apart. If you are going to frost the cookies, leave them plain. You can sprinkle the other cookies with colored sugar or sprinkle after applying a light coating of beaten egg white. (Use the egg white that you separated from the yolk in the recipe).

Bake for 7 to 10 minutes or until the top is light brown. Watch you do not burn the bottoms. Cool and frost or serve.

Variations: Add 1/2 cup slivered almonds to the cookies before chilling the dough.

ROLLED SCOTCH SHORTBREAD

This cookie is very dense and rich. Only use real butter to make it because that is what gives it the richness. There is only 3 ingredients in this recipe and it makes about 2 dozen cookies.

Ingredients:
2 cups butter softened
1 cup brown sugar tightly packed
4-1/2 cups all-purpose flour

Directions:
Preheat your oven to 325 degrees and prepare cookie sheets by covering with parchment paper.

Cream the softened butter and the brown sugar in the mixer and start adding flour a little at a time. Add up to 3-3/4 cups of the flour and remove the bowl from the mixer scraping the beater down. You should have a soft dough. Sprinkle the rest of the flour on a board. Scoop the dough out of the mixing bowl and place it on the floured board and start kneading for 5 minutes, incorporating enough of the flour on the board to make an elastic but soft dough. Roll with a rolling pin to a thickness of 1/2 inch. Use a sharp knife to cut into 3 inch wide strips and cut into 1 inch sections. Prick each section with a fork and place on cookies sheets.

Bake for 20 to 25 minutes or until the shortbread sections turn a light golden brown and cool on racks.

Variation: I would not add anything to the cookie recipe. The ingredients are measured and if anything is off the cookie will either spread all over or become hard like a rock. To vary the cookie, you can drizzle with a glaze. Make a lemon glaze by mixing enough fresh lemon juice and about 1 teaspoon lemon zest to confectioner's sugar to make a thin consistency.

ROLLED CHOCOLATE CUT OUT COOKIES

These cookies have a chocolaty flavor and they are also brown in color so they make for great football cookies or animal cookies. You can frost these or drizzle with a chocolate glaze. They taste marvelous plain too. This recipe makes 3 dozen cookies.

Ingredients:
3 cups all-purpose flour
1 teaspoon baking powder
10 tablespoons unsweetened cocoa powder
1/4 teaspoon salt
1 cup of butter or shortening
2 cups of granulated sugar
3 eggs
2-1/2 teaspoons vanilla

Directions:
Whisk the flour baking powder, cocoa powder and salt in a medium bowl and set aside. Cream the butter or shortening and sugar in your mixer until it is smooth and light. Add each egg, one at a time, beating in after every addition. Add the vanilla and beat well. Add the dry ingredients to the creamed mixture a little at a time until it is all mixed in. Scrape this dough onto a square of wax paper and wrap it up placing it in the refrigerator for at least 2 hours.

Preheat the oven to 350 degrees F and prepare cookie sheets by placing parchment paper on them.

Separate the dough into 2 halves and take one leaving the other in the refrigerator. Place the dough onto a lightly floured board and roll out to 1/4 inch thick. Cut with cookie cutters and place on prepared cookie sheets.

Bake for 10 to 12 minutes and remove from oven. Let cool on racks about 2 minutes and remove to cooling racks. Continue with other half of dough.

Variation: Place mini chocolate chips on the cookies while still hot on the cooling racks. You can make them chocolate mint cookies by using 1-1/4 teaspoons vanilla and 1 – 1/4 teaspoons mint flavoring.

CUT OUT PUMPKIN COOKIES

These cookies have the fall flavor of orange and pumpkin and can be enhanced further with frosting, a vanilla drizzle or studded with candy corn. The recipe makes anywhere between 1 to 2 dozen cookies depending on the size of your pumpkin shaped cookie cutter.

Ingredients:
2-1/4 cups all-purpose flour
1/4 teaspoon ground cinnamon
1/4 teaspoon ground ginger
1/4 teaspoon ground nutmeg
1/8 teaspoon ground cloves
1/8 teaspoon salt

3/4 cup of unsalted butter (do not use regular butter or margarine or they will be too salty.
1/2 cup brown sugar packed tightly
1-1/2 tablespoon orange zest from a fresh orange
1/2 cup pumpkin puree
1 egg yolk (save the white)
1 teaspoon vanilla

Directions:
Whisk the flour, spices and salt in a medium bowl until well combined and set aside. In your mixer, cream the butter that has been softened with the brown sugar and orange zest. Add in the puree and mix well. Add the egg yolk and vanilla and mix well. Add the dry ingredients gradually to the butter mixture mixing it in well after each addition. Form the dough into a ball and place it in plastic wrap. Refrigerate the dough for at least 30 minutes.

Preheat your oven to 375 degrees and prepare some cookie sheets by covering with parchment paper.

Roll the dough 1/8 inch thick on a floured board. Cut with cookie cutters and place on the parchment covered cookie sheets spacing about 1 inch apart. Bake the cookies for about 10 to 12 minutes. Remove immediately to cooling racks. If you are decorating with candy corn or chocolate chips, brush the cookies lightly with whisked egg white and place them on the cookies while they are hot so they stick better. You can also frost with vanilla frosting or drizzle with chocolate glaze.

Variations: Add a maple flavoring instead of vanilla.

BROWN SUGAR CUT OUT COOKIES

This is an old recipe that makes many cookies. Depending on the size of your cookie cutter, it makes about 7 dozen cookies that are delicious. You have to ice these cookies and I have included the recipe for the icing that can be used for any cookie. Note that there are no eggs in this recipe.

Ingredients:
1 cup softened butter
2 cups brown sugar packed tightly
1 -1/2 teaspoon vanilla
5 cups all-purpose flour
1/4 teaspoon salt
1 teaspoon baking soda
1/4 cup milk
1 more cup softened butter
1 more teaspoon vanilla
confectioner's sugar

milk

Directions:
In your mixer mix the butter, brown sugar and vanilla until creamy. In another bowl whisk together the flour, salt and baking soda until it is combined well. Add the flour mixture slowly to the butter mixture mixing well after each addition. When the dough starts to get a little dry, add the milk a little at a time. The dough should be soft. Form into a ball and refrigerate for at least 1 hour.

Preheat your oven to 350 degrees and cover cookie sheets with parchment paper. You can reuse your parchment paper up until it starts to get too greasy. I've used one piece 3 times before I had to change it.

Pull off a chunk of the dough and roll it out on a floured board to 1/4 inch thick. Keep the rest of the dough in the refrigerator until time to use. Cut with cookie cutters and place at least 2 inches apart on the cookie sheets. Repeat with rest of the dough.

Bake cookies for about 6 minutes or until lightly brown. Cool on cookie sheets about 2 minutes and remove to cooling racks.

To make the icing cream the butter in the mixture with the vanilla until smooth. Gradually add in confectioner's sugar about 1/2 cup at a time and a splash of milk until you get a light and fluffy icing. You may use 1-1/2 cups, 2 or more. Spread on cooled cookies.

Variation: Instead of vanilla use maple extract and add the maple extract into the icing. You can also use lemon or orange extract for a different flavor.

CORNMEAL COOKIES

This is another very old recipe that comes from the south. It uses cornmeal and that makes these cookies very crunchy indeed. Only use real butter with this recipe or the cookies will have little flavor. The recipe makes approximately 2 dozen delicious cookies.

Ingredients:
1-1/2 cups all-purpose flour
1/2 cup cornmeal (use yellow or white)
1 teaspoon baking powder
1/4 teaspoon salt
3/4 cup butter that has been softened
3/4 cup granulated sugar
1 egg
1-1/2 teaspoons vanilla
1/2 cup golden raisins

Directions:
Whisk together the flour, cornmeal, baking powder and salt in a medium bowl and set aside. Cream the butter and sugar in your mixer until it is smooth and fluffy. Add the egg and beat it in very well. Add the cornmeal mixture to the butter mixture gradually to the butter mixture beating in well after each addition. Add the vanilla and combine well. Hand mix in the golden raisins. Form into a ball and wrap in plastic wrap. Place the dough in the refrigerator for 1 hour or more.

Preheat your oven to 350 degrees and prepare cookie sheets with parchment paper. Spray the paper with non-stick spray.

Flour a board and roll the refrigerated dough out to about 1/4 inch thickness. If you have a small board, do this in two batches keeping the unused batch wrapped and in the refrigerator. Cut with 2-1/2 inch diameter round cookie cutters and place on the cookie sheets about 1 inch apart.

Bake for 10 to 12 minutes or until the edges become golden brown.

Variation: Use regular raisins, dried currants or dried cranberries instead of golden raisins.

CHOCOLATE ORANGE SHORTBREAD CUT OUT COOKIES

This cookie gives a new twist to shortbread. It has the flavor of chocolate and orange, which really goes well together. The recipe makes 2-1/2 dozen and they do freeze well.

Ingredients:
1 -1/2 sticks softened unsalted butter (12 tablespoons)
1/2 cup + 2 tablespoons granulated sugar
1 -1/2 teaspoon vanilla
1 tablespoon orange zest
1 cup all-purpose flour
1/4 teaspoon salt
3/4 cup unsweetened cocoa powder

Place the butter in a mixer with the granulated sugar and beat until smooth and creamy. Add the vanilla and the orange zest and mix in well. Place the flour and salt in a medium bowl. Use a sifter or fine sieve to sift the cocoa powder into the flour mixture. Cocoa tends to clump and this will prevent this from happening. Whisk well and add gradually to the butter mixture until it is completely mixed in. Form dough into a ball and put it in the refrigerator for about 1 hour.

Preheat the oven to 325 degrees F and line cookie sheets with parchment paper. Place another square of parchment paper on the counter, unwrap the dough and place it in the middle. Place another square of parchment paper over top and roll out to about 1/4 inch thick. You do not want to add flour to this cookie while rolling or it will become tough. The parchment paper will keep the dough from sticking.

Cut the dough with cookie cutters and place each one 1 inch apart on the cookie sheets. Bake for 13 to 15 minutes until the cookie is firm. Cool on the cookie sheets for 5 minutes and remove to a cooling rack.

Variation: You can make a simple vanilla drizzle with confectioners' sugar and milk and drizzle it over the top of the cookies, or make orange drizzle by adding orange juice and orange zest instead of milk.

WELSH COOKIES

These are the smallest bite of heaven on earth there is. Welsh cookies are actually a small flaky cookie that tastes a bit like pie dough with currents in them. These do not keep long, but you shouldn't have to worry about that. Cut them out with a small 1/2 to 1 inch diameter round cookie cutter. It should make about 3 to 5 dozen depending on the size of your cutter.

Ingredients:
2 cups all-purpose flour
3/4 cups granulated sugar + more for dipping
1/2 teaspoon baking soda
pinch of salt
1/2 cup softened butter (do not use anything else)
1/2 cup dried currants
1/4 cup buttermilk
1 egg
1/2 teaspoon vanilla

Directions:
Preheat your oven to 350 degrees and cover a few cookie sheets with parchment paper.

Combine the flour, sugar, baking soda and salt in a large bowl and whisk until well blended. Add the butter and cut in like pie crust with a pastry cutter or two knives until the mixture looks like coarse meal. Stir the currants in with a wooden spoon.

In a small bowl combine the buttermilk, egg and vanilla and beat well with a fork. Make a well in the center of the flour mixture and pour the liquid ingredients in. Using the fork, combine some of the flour mixture into the well with the liquid ingredients and keep mixing it in until it is completely combined. You might need to use your hands at the end and you might need a little more buttermilk if the dough is stiff. You should have a soft dough.

Flour a board and shape the dough into a ball kneading it on the board about 5 to 6 times. Roll with a rolling pin to 1/4 inch thick. Have a small bowl of granulated sugar ready and cut the small circles dipping them in the sugar so that both sides get some on them. Place them on the cookie sheets and bake 10 to 12 minutes or until the cookies get slightly brown. Remove to a cooling rack immediately.

Variation: Some find rolling the rounds in sugar to make the cookie too sweet. You can omit this if you would like. You can also go very authentic and add 1/4 cup caraway seeds to the mix when you add the currants.

MORAVIAN SPICE COOKIES

The Moravians came to America from Germany in 1735 and took in German immigrants, Native Americans and African Slaves. The church is actually one of the oldest protestant churches in the world and the German church is just one branch. The Moravians had a large German population in Pennsylvania and these cookies were some of their favorite confections. Germans are known for spicy sweets and this is not different. These cookies are dark brown from the molasses and have pepper in them for extra spice. They are usually cut in rounds and the most notable thing about them is that they are wafer thin. Bakers pride themselves on being able to make the thinnest cookie. This recipe makes about 2 to 3 dozen depending on the size of the cutter and the dough can be rolled out, rolled onto wax paper, put in a freezer bag and frozen. You will be very surprised at what is in these cookies.

Ingredients:
1-2/3 cup of all-purpose flour
1/4 teaspoon salt
1/4 teaspoon baking soda
1/2 teaspoon baking powder
1/4 teaspoon ground ginger
1/4 teaspoon ground cloves
1 teaspoon ground cinnamon
1/4 teaspoon ground nutmeg
1/2 teaspoon white pepper
1/2 teaspoon ground mustard (this is mustard is in the spice section and dry, not wet mustard you put on hot dogs)
3/4 cup brown sugar packed tight
6 tablespoons softened butter (only butter)
1/4 cup dark molasses
1 egg yolk

Directions:

Whisk the flour and rest of the dry ingredients in a large bowl combining it well and set the bowl aside. Beat the brown sugar and butter in your mixer until it is well creamed. Add the molasses and the egg yolk and beat well to combine. Set aside. Gradually beat the dry ingredients into the butter mixture a little at a time making sure each addition is well mixed. The dough will not be smooth and elastic, but will be loose and slightly crumbling almost as if there is not enough moisture in it.

Form the dough into a mound with your hands. Take 1/3 of this dough and put it on top of piece of parchment paper. Use your hands to pat it into a rectangle. Put another piece of parchment on top and with your rolling pin, roll as thin as you can. The prescribed thickness is 1/16 of an inch, but that is going to take some practice. Repeat with all the dough. Hint: Place the bottom parchment on a large flat cookie sheet and roll on that so you have a hard surface and you do not have to lift the dough off a hard surface for the next step.

Remove the top layer of parchment paper, replace with clean paper and set the dough in a freezer for 30 minutes.

Preheat your oven to 325 degrees and prepare more cookie sheets with parchment paper.

Take the dough from the freezer and remove the top parchment paper (use this to line your baking cookie sheets. Immediately cut into 2 inch rounds and place on prepared cookie sheets. Freeze cut outs for 15 minutes and sprinkle the tops with a cinnamon and sugar mixture before putting them in the oven. Bake for 8 to 10 minutes and watch carefully. The cookies will be dark brown, but they burn quickly. Once you see the edges starting to get brown, take them out. Let them sit 2 minutes before removing from the cookie sheet and placing them on cooling racks.

Variations: I would not vary this recipe except for placing a thin sliced almond on top of each cookie before baking.

ALMOND BISCOTTI COOKIES

Biscotti is a rather hard cookie that is meant to be dunked into coffee or other liquid drinks in order to soften them up to eat. They come from Italy and are made in many flavors. This Almond biscotti cookie is especially good with coffee and although it isn't rolled with a rolling pin, the dough is rolled into a log, baked and then cut in slices. It then goes back into the oven to dry the cookie out.

Ingredients:
2 -3/4 cups all-purpose flour
1/4 teaspoon salt
1-1/2 teaspoons baking powder
1/2 cup butter

1-1/4 cup granulated sugar
3 eggs
2 teaspoons almond extract
1-1/2 cup finely chopped roasted almonds

Directions:
Whisk together the flour, salt and baking powder and set the bowl aside. Cream the butter and sugar in a mixer bowl and add the eggs one at a time beating in every time. Add the almond extract. Gradually add the flour mixture to the creamed mixture until it is all incorporated. Hand beat in the chopped almonds. Cover and refrigerate the dough overnight or at least 2 hours.

Preheat your oven to 350 degrees and cover two baking sheets with parchment paper. Divide the dough in half and shape into two logs about 12 by 2 inches. Place on the cookie sheets and bake about 25 to 30 minutes or until golden and firm. Place on a cooling rack for 15 minutes.

Use a serrated knife to cut 1/2 inch thick slices and place on parchment covered baking sheets in a single layer. Keep baking until the cookies are dry and crisp. This will take 18 to 22 minutes. Cool on the baking sheet and remove to airtight containers when cool.

Variations: Use vanilla extract instead of almond extract. Add 1/2 teaspoon cinnamon to the mix for a spicy cookie. Try using lemon or orange flavoring instead of vanilla and add 1/2 teaspoon lemon or orange zest.

DATE PINWHEEL COOKIES

These cookies are spiraled with a prune and nut filling that is delicious. The recipe makes about 5 dozen and the dough is easily frozen after it is rolled up. This is an old time recipe that many people made for holidays, but it became a regular staple of the household because they are very easy to make.

Ingredients:
2-1/2 cups all-purpose flour
1/2 teaspoon baking soda
1/4 teaspoon salt
1/3 cup softened butter
1/3 cup sugar
1 large egg
1/2 cup honey
1-1/4 teaspoon of lemon flavoring

Filling:
1-1/2 cup chopped walnuts
1/2 cup diced prunes pitted
1/4 cup granulated sugar

1-1/2 teaspoon ground cinnamon
1 egg
1 teaspoon orange rind

Directions:
Place the flour, baking soda and salt in a bowl and whisk it until well combined. In your mixer place the butter and sugar and cream well. Beat in the egg, honey and lemon flavoring. Gradually add the flour mixture a little at a time, beating well after each time it is added. The dough should be soft and you may need another 1/4 cup to make it so it isn't so sticky. Wrap the dough in plastic wrap and place in the refrigerator for 2 hours or overnight.

In a food processor chop the walnuts until they are fine. Add prunes, sugar, cinnamon, egg and rind and process until a paste forms.

Divide the dough in half and roll out one half on a lightly floured surface to an 8 inch square that is 1/4 inch thick. Spread half of the filling on the dough but leave 1/8 inch around the edges. Roll the dough jelly-roll style and press long edge to seal. Wrap with plastic wrap and refrigerate again for 2 hours or overnight. Do the same with the other part of the dough.

Preheat your oven to 350 degrees F and prepare cookie sheets with parchment paper sprayed lightly with non-stick spray. Unwrap the rolls and cut into 1/4 inch slices placing them flat on the cookie sheets about 1 inch apart. Bake for 10 to 12 minutes or until they are brown and firm. Cool on racks immediately.

Variation: Use dates instead of prunes and almonds instead of walnuts.

RASPBERRY SPIRALS

These cookies are rolled jelly roll style and are deliciously fruity. This recipe makes about 3 dozen cookies and this dough is also easy to freeze while it is in the roll.

Ingredients:
1/2 cup softened butter
1 cup granulated sugar
1 egg
1 teaspoon vanilla
3-3/4 cup all-purpose flour
1 teaspoon baking powder
1/4 teaspoon salt
1/4 cup seedless raspberry jam
2 tablespoons more sugar (Use red colored sugar if desired)

Directions:

In your mixer cream the butter and sugar until it becomes light. Add the egg and the vanilla and beat well. In another bowl, whisk the flour, baking powder and salt. Add the dry mixture to the butter mixer one tablespoon at a time until it is well combined. You should have a soft dough. Wrap the dough and place in the refrigerator for 1 hour.

Remove the plastic wrap and place the dough on a floured board. Roll into a 12 by 9 inch rectangle that is about 1/4 inch thick. Spread the jam on the surface and sprinkle a little sugar over top. Roll jelly roll style and press down the long edge to seal. Wrap in plastic wrap again and put in the refrigerator 2 hours or overnight.

Preheat the oven to 350 degrees F and prepare cookie sheets by covering with parchment paper.

Cut the dough into 1/4 inch slices and place flat on the cookie sheets about 1 inch apart. Bake for 10 to 13 minutes or until the cookies become light brown. Cool on the cookie sheet for 5 minutes and remove to cooling racks.

Variation: You can use any kind of jam you would like. Peach, blackberry, strawberry and even grape is good.

FILLED AND ROLLED ANISE COOKIES

Anise is slightly licorice in flavor and it combines with the prunes and chocolate to make for an interesting flavor. Some of the things in these cookies are very unusual, but delicious when put together. This recipe makes about 2 dozen cookies and you really have to keep them away from other baked goods because the anise flavor and scent will tend to rub off. The cookie is somewhat like a fruit cake with anise added to the mix.

Ingredients:
1/2 cup melted shortening
2 cups flour
2 teaspoons baking powder
3 large eggs
1/2 cup sugar
2 teaspoons anise extract
1 pound prunes that have been pitted
1 tablespoon honey
2 tablespoons fruit cocktail that comes in a can and has been chopped
1/4 cup semi-sweet chocolate chips

Directions:
Preheat your oven to 375 degrees and prepare cookie sheets by covering with parchment paper. This is different because you bake the cookies in the roll and cut them when they come out of the oven and are cool.

Melt the shortening in a heavy pan on the stove or in a microwave safe glass bowl in the microwave. Meanwhile, combine the flour and baking powder in a medium bowl and whisk to combine. Set this mixture aside. In your mixer, beat the eggs with the sugar until it is creamy. Add the melted shortening in a stream while continuing to beat. Running it in a stream cools it down a bit so that it won't cook and curdle the eggs.

Add the dry ingredients to the ingredients in the mixture gradually until it is all well combined. Add the anise extract and mix in. Scrape the dough onto a floured board and roll it out to a 10 by 12 inch rectangle.

Place the prunes, honey, fruit cocktail and chocolate chips in a heavy pan and cook over medium heat until it is bubbly and slightly thickened. Remove from the stove and let it cool about 15 minutes. Spread the filling over the rectangle about 2 inches from each edge. Roll the dough jelly roll style and place it on the baking sheet.

Bake 15 to 20 minutes or until browned and firm. Remove from the oven and transfer to a cooling rack. Once the cookies are cool, cut them into diagonal slices about 1/2 inch thick.

Variation: If you like a little crunch with your cookie, sprinkle about 1/3 cup chopped walnuts, pecans or almonds on top before you roll it up.

CREAM CHEESE JAMMIES

This cookie recipe is so easy your won't believe how great they taste. They have a tangy cream cheese flavor along with any flavor jam you choose to use. This recipe makes about 2 to 3 dozen cookies depending on how thick you cut them.

Ingredients:
1/2 pound softened cream cheese
1/2 pound softened butter (don't use anything else)
2 cups flour
Jam
Granulated sugar

Directions:
Beat the cream cheese and butter until creamy and smooth. Gradually add the flour starting out very slow and increasing speed as it is incorporated into the dough. Divide the dough into 3 sections and wrap in plastic warp. Refrigerate the dough overnight.

Preheat your oven to 350 degrees and place parchment paper on several cookie sheets that have been sprayed with non stick spray.

Take out one section of the dough and roll it out on a floured board to a rectangle that is about 1/8 inch thick. Spread the jam to 1 inch of the edges. Spread a generous amount of jam on but not too thick because it will just ooze out if you put too much on. Sprinkle with a light coat of sugar and roll jelly roll fashion. Cut in 3/4 inch slices and place them flat on the cookie sheets about 1 inch apart. Continue with the other two sections.

Bake for 15 minutes and check the cookies. They need to be lightly browned and puffed so you may have to go another 5 minutes. They tend to burn easily so keep an eye on them. Remove from the oven and place on cooling racks.

Variation: Use any jam you like including peach, apricot, strawberry, grape, rhubarb/strawberry and add a sprinkle of nuts if you would like some crunch before you roll them.

Chapter 5: Excellent Filled and Sandwich Cookies

Some of these filled and sandwich cookies might also be rolled out and cut with cookie cutters, however, they are assembled instead of rolled jelly roll style and cut or two cookies contain a delicious filling. This filling might include jam. These cookies are a little bit more intensive in making, but they are so worth it when it comes to flavor. Some of these cookies are also filled in other ways to make treats with a surprise inside.

LINZER TART COOKIES

Linz is a large city in Austria famous for their Linzertortes, which is a buttery torte filled with black current jam and has an almond flavor. The Linzertorte is the oldest known torte of its kind with the recipe from the early 1600s. The cookie is a smaller version. It is a round or heart shaped cookie with raspberry preserves on top. Another cookie that is cut out in the middle to expose the jam is placed on top and it is usually dusted with powder sugar. This recipe only makes 12 full cookies, but they are a special treat that take some time to make.

Ingredients:
2 cups all-purpose flour
1-1/3 cups ground almonds
1/4 teaspoon ground cinnamon
1-1/4 cups unsalted butter that has been softened (only use unsalted butter)
2/3 cup granulated sugar
5 tablespoons raspberry jam
1/3 cup confectioners' sugar

Directions:
Whisk together the flour, ground almonds and cinnamon in a medium bowl and set aside. In your mixer bowl, beat the butter and sugar until it becomes creamy and fluffy. Gradually add the flour mixture to the butter mixture by tablespoonfuls until it is all combined. The mixture is somewhat stiff.

Divide the dough in half and shape into two balls. Wrap in plastic wrap and refrigerate for one hour.

Preheat your oven to 325 degrees F and prepare baking sheets by covering with parchment paper.

Roll one ball of dough out on a floured board to about 1/8 inch thick. Use a 2-1/2 inch round cookie cutter to cut 12 circles from the dough. You will probably have to use the scraps and knead them together and roll out to get all 12 circles. Place cut out circles on cookie sheets about 1 inch apart and place in refrigerator to keep cool while doing the same with the other ball of dough.

Once the other ball of dough has been rolled and cut into 12 more circles, use a 1/2 inch round cookie cutter to cut out the center of the circle.

Bake about 10 to 15 minutes until light brown. Cool on the cookie sheet about 10 minutes and transfer to cooling racks until completely cool.

Spread jam on the plain round cookies and set the cookie with the cut out center on top. Lightly press together. Take a teaspoon and spoon a little more jam into the hole. Sprinkle with confectioners' sugar.

Variation: You can use any flavor jam you like. Try peach, apricot and strawberry for different flavors. If you don't like almond flavoring, you can use vanilla instead.

EMPIRE COOKIES

These are also often called English or Scottish tea cookies. They have a sweet flavor and are rolled, cut in rounds and spread with jam. The recipe only makes 12 cookies, but that is because the longer they sit, the soggier they get. Make sure you make them for a party so they will be eaten up in a day or so.

Ingredients:
2 cups all-purpose flour
1 teaspoon baking powder
1/2 cup softened butter
1/2 cup granulated sugar
1 egg
1-1/4 teaspoon vanilla
1/2 cup jam
1 cup confectioners' sugar
1/4 teaspoon almond extract
1 tablespoon hot water
1/4 cup candied cherries or apricots that have been chopped

Directions:
Preheat the oven to 350 degrees and cover baking sheets with parchment paper.

Whisk the flour and baking powder in a bowl and set aside. Cream the butter with the sugar in your mixer and beat in the egg and vanilla. Gradually add the flour mixture to the butter mixture making sure it is well combined.

Flour a board and roll the dough to 1/8 inch thick. Use 2 inch round cookie cutters to cut 24 rounds. Bake for 10 minutes or until they start to brown at the edges. Cool on racks thoroughly.

Take half of the cooled cookies and spread with your favorite jam and top with another cookie pressing down lightly. In a small bowl combine the confectioners' sugar, extract and hot water and whisk until creamy and the consistency to be able to drizzle it over the cookie. Top with a small piece of cherry or apricot.

Variation: If you are using orange marmalade as a filling, use a citrus flavored extract instead of vanilla.

HAMANTASHEN

Hamantashen or Haman's hats are a Jewish recipe for a jam filled cookie that is distinct because of its triangular shape resembling a hat. They are traditionally served at Purim. In the book of Esther, Haman offered money to Ahasuerus in order that he could destroy the Jews, but Queen Esther foils his plans. These are often filled with poppyseed filling, date and all kinds of jams and pie filling. This recipe makes about 17 cookies.

Ingredients:
5-1/2 cups all-purpose flour
3 teaspoons baking powder
1/4 teaspoon salt
4 eggs
1 cup vegetable oil
1-1/4 cup granulated sugar
2 teaspoons vanilla
1 can apple pie filling or 1 jar jam

Directions:
Whisk together the flour, baking powder and salt in a large bowl and set aside. In the mixer beat the eggs and add the oil. Mix in the sugar and vanilla. Add the flour mixture to the egg mixture gradually until it is all incorporated. Form the dough into a ball, wrap in plastic wrap and refrigerate 2 hours or overnight.

Preheat the oven to 350 degrees F and cover cookie sheets with parchment paper.

Remove the dough from the refrigerator and knead it until it become soft. Flour a board and roll the dough to about 1/4 inch. Use a 3 inch diameter round cookie cutter to cut out circles. Place 1 tablespoon of pie filling or jam in the middle of the circle. Fold up the edges making a triangular form. You do not want to totally cover the pie filling or jam, just contain it in the triangle. Place on baking sheets and bake for about 20 minutes or until the edges get brown. Remove to cooling racks to cool.

Variation: Use any kind of pie filling or jam to make these.

BUTTERY JAM COOKIES

The buttery flavor of these cookies along with the fruity jam makes for a favorite in any family. This recipe makes 36 delicious cookies and they are so easy to make.

Ingredients:
3/4 cup softened butter
1/2 cup granulated sugar
2 egg yolks
1-3/4 cup all-purpose flour
1/2 cup jam

In your mixer cream the butter and sugar until light and fluffy. Add the egg yolks, one a time, mixing well after each one. Gradually add the flour by tablespoonful's until it is all incorporated into the dough. You should have a soft dough. Put plastic wrap over the opening of the bowl and refrigerate for 1 hour.

Preheat your oven to 375 degrees F and line cookie sheets with parchment paper.

Dip out 1 teaspoon of the dough and roll it into a 1 inch ball and place on the cookie sheet 1 inch apart. Use fingers to make a depression in the top of the cookie that does not go all the way through to the cookie sheet. Fill this hole with 1/2 teaspoon of the jam.

Bake for 8 to 10 minutes until brown on the bottom. Remove immediately to cool on cooling racks.

Variation: Sprinkle each cookie with a little granulated sugar to make them sparkle and give a little extra sweetness. They don't really need it though.

AUSTRIAN PEACH LOOK ALIKE COOKIES

These cookies have apricot jam, chocolate chips, pecans and rum in them. Be prepared for a spectacular cookie suitable for special occasions, like parties or a wedding. This recipe only makes 6 cookies and that is because they are so rich. They are made with apricot jam, so you are probably wondering why they are called peach cookies. It is because they look like peaches. The cookies are actually a sandwich cookie that you put together to look like a peach. You can even enhance them with little plastic green stems, found in the cake decorating part of your craft store, at the top.

Ingredients:
3-3/4 cups all-purpose flour
1 teaspoon baking powder
3/4 cup unsalted buttermilk
1 cup granulated sugar
2 eggs

1-1/4 teaspoons vanilla
Filling:
1/4 cup semi-sweet chocolate chips
2/3 cup apricot jam
1/3 cup ground pecans
2 teaspoons rum
Finishing
1/4 cup water
1 cup granulated sugar
2 drops red food coloring
4 drops yellow food coloring
Plastic disposable gloves (you will definitely need these)

Directions:
Preheat your oven to 325 degrees and prepare cookie sheets by covering with parchment paper.

Whisk together the flour and baking soda in a large bowl and set it aside. In your mixer cream the butter and 1 cup granulated sugar until it is light. Beat one egg in and then the other and add the vanilla. Gradually start to add the flour mixture alternately with the milk until it is all combined.

Take dough by rounded teaspoonful's and roll into a 1 inch ball. Place the balls 1 inch apart on the covered cookie sheets. Bake for 15 to 20 minutes or until the cookies start to brown on the bottom. Remove from baking sheets and cool on cooling racks.

Once the cookies are cool, flip them over and take a sharp pairing knife to carve a little hole in the under, or flat side of the cookie. Do not throw away the crumbs. In a microwave safe bowl, melt the semi-sweet chocolate chips on medium 1 minute at a time, stirring after each time until they are melted. Stir until smooth. Pour into a bowl and add the jam, pecans, rum and the saved crumbs from the cookies. Fill the holes in the bottoms of each cookie and place the flat side of one cookie against the flat side of another to make a peach shape. The filling should be adequately sticky to keep the two halves together. If they don't stick, add a little more filling in between.

Divide the finishing granulated sugar with 1/4 cup in one small bowl and 3/4 cup in another. Drop the drops of red coloring in the 1/4 cup bowl and wearing gloves, rub the sugar between your fingers to color it red. Do the same with the yellow coloring and the 3/4 cup sugar. Take a pinch of the red sugar and add it to the yellow and mix well with the fingers. This will help it attain a peach color.

Brush each cookie with water and roll them in the yellow sugar and dip part of it in the red to make it look like a peach. Insert the little plastic green stem and let them sit on wax paper for about an hour before putting them in a tin.

KIFLI

Kifli is a Hungarian cookie that is filled with walnuts and rolled in a crescent shape. Sometimes they are also filled with an apricot or raspberry filling. This recipe makes about 24 servings. The dough is extremely sticky and making them on a rainy day makes them even more gooey, so try to make them on a dry day if you don't have air conditioning.

Ingredients:
2-1/2 cups all-purpose flour
1/4 teaspoon salt
1/2 teaspoon baking powder
9 ounces cream cheese that has been softened
1 cup of butter that has been softened
3 egg yolks (save the whites)
1-1/2 teaspoon vanilla
3 egg whites (from the yolks)
1 cup granulated sugar
8 ounces ground walnuts
1/3 cup confectioners' sugar

Directions:
Whisk the flour, salt and baking powder together in a large bowl and set aside. In your mixer cream the butter and cream cheese until fluffy. Add the egg yolks and vanilla and combine well. Add the flour mixture gradually mixing well after each addition. Flour your hands and divide the dough into 5 equal pieces. Wrap each piece in plastic and store in the refrigerator overnight.

In the mixing bowl beat the egg whites until they begin to form soft peaks. Add a little granulated sugar at a time until the mixture forms stiff peaks. Remove the bowl from the mixer and using a spatula, fold in the ground walnuts until just mixed in. Set this mixture aside.

Flour a board and take one of the pieces of dough from the refrigerator. Roll the dough out to 1/4 inch thickness and cut it into 3 inch squares with a sharp knife. Place 1/2 teaspoon of the walnut mixture in the center and roll up from one side to the other. Pinch it into a crescent shape and place on a parchment covered cookie sheet about 1 inch apart. Place the cookie sheet in the refrigerator until the dough becomes firm and cold. Do the same with all the other portions of the dough.

Preheat your oven to 350 degrees while the cookies are in the refrigerator. Bake for 10 to 12 minutes or until they are a light brown. Remove to a cooling rack. Once the cookies are cool, place the confectioners' sugar in a bowl and roll each cookie in it.

Variations: Add 1/4 teaspoon cinnamon to the egg white and walnut mixture to give it a little extra punch of spice.

SWEDISH INSPIRED CREAM WAFERS

These cookies are a sandwich cookie filled with a cream between some flaky cookies. This recipe makes 30 whole cookies that will fly off the serving dish when you make them.

Ingredients:
1/3 cup heavy whipping cream
1 cup softened butter
2 cups all-purpose flour
1/3 cup granulated sugar
Filling:
1/4 cup softened butter
3/4 cup confectioners' sugar
1 egg yolk
1 teaspoon vanilla
red food coloring

Directions:
To make the cookies pour the cream into the mixer bowl and add the softened butter. Beat slowly until it is well combined. Add the flour, a little at a time until it is all combined and makes a soft dough. Form into a ball and wrap in plastic wrap. Chill in the refrigerator for at least 1 hour.

Preheat your oven to 375 degrees and prepare your cookie sheets by covering them with parchment paper.

Flour a board and separate the dough into three equal sections. Take the first and roll it out to 1/8 inch thick. Place the other two sections back in the refrigerator until it is time to roll them. Take a sheet of wax paper and sprinkle the granulated sugar on it. Cut the dough with a 1-1/2 inch diameter round cookie cutter. Place on the wax paper with the sugar and make sure each side gets well covered with sugar. Place the rounds on the prepared cookie sheet about 1 inch apart and poke with a fork 4 times. Repeat this with all the dough.

Bake the rounds for 7 to 9 minutes transferring immediately to a wire rack when done.

Make the filling by placing the 1/4 cup butter, confectioners' sugar, yolk and vanilla in the mixer and beating it together until it is very creamy like a frosting. Add a few drops of red or any other color food coloring if desired. Spread a little bit of this cream on one of the cookies and top with another.

Variation: Use lemon extract and put a 1 teaspoon of real lemon juice in the cream for a creamy lemon experience.

RAISIN FILLED COOKIES

This is a very old recipe that is very sweet and delicious. You drop the raisin filling in the middle of one cookie and cover with another then bake. There are many different variations with this recipe and it make about 3 dozen cookies.

Ingredients:
6 cups all-purpose flour
1 teaspoon salt
4 teaspoons baking powder
2 teaspoons baking soda
1 cup butter or margarine
2 cups granulated sugar
2 eggs
1 cup milk
2 teaspoons vanilla

Filling:
1 cup granulated sugar
3 tablespoons cornstarch
1-1/2 cups water, divided
1-1/2 teaspoons real lemon juice
1-15 ounce box raisins

Directions:
Whisk together in a large bowl the flour, salt, baking powder and baking soda. Set this mixture aside. Cream the sugar and margarine or butter together in your mixer until light. Add the eggs, one at a time and mix in well. In a large measuring cup measure the milk and add the vanilla to it. Gradually add the flour mixture alternately with the milk mixture until all is combined making a soft dough that is very sticky. Cover the mixer bowl with plastic wrap and refrigerate it for about 1 hour.

Meantime, make the filling by whisking together the sugar, cornstarch and 1/4 cup water in a medium saucepan to make a paste-like substance while heating over medium high heat. Add the rest of the water, the lemon juice and the raisins. Continue to cook over medium heat and stir frequently until the mixture starts to bubble and thickens. The raisins should get very plump. This should take about 5 to 10 minutes. Cool to room temperature.

Preheat the oven to 400 degrees F and cover baking sheets with parchment paper.

Cut the dough into three equal sections and put the other two back in the refrigerator until ready to use. Place the section of dough on a floured board and roll to 1/8 inch thick. You will need a great deal of flour because the dough is so sticky. Cut with 2-1/2 to 2-3/4 inch round cookie cutter. Place them on baking sheet about 1 inch apart and fill them by placing 1-1/2 teaspoon of the cooled filling in the middle of each cookie. Cut more circles out and place them on top of each cookie with filling. Just lightly press edges with a form. Repeat with all the dough and the filling. Cut a slit in the top of each cookie or punch it twice with a fork.

Bake for 15 minutes or until the cookies are a light golden brown on top. Cool on the cookie sheet 10 minutes and transfer to a cooling rack to cool. These will last about 5 days if kept in an airtight container and if you can keep them that long.

Variations: Use dried apricots and orange juice instead of raisins and lemon juice. You will have to cut the apricots into small pieces that are raisin size. Make the cookie spicy by adding 1/4 teaspoon ground cinnamon, 1/8 teaspoon ground allspice, 1/4 teaspoon ground cloves to the flour mixture before mixing it in.

CHERRY PIE COOKIES

It looks like these cookies are really hard to make, but they aren't and they make a great impression. They look exactly like miniature cherry pies. This recipe makes about 5 dozen of the lattice look cherry pies.

Ingredients:
1-3/4 cup all-purpose flour
1/2 teaspoon baking soda
1/8 teaspoon salt
1/2 cup softened butter
1 cup granulated sugar
1 egg
1/2 teaspoon vanilla
2/3 cup more softened butter
5 cups confectioners' sugar
1 teaspoon more vanilla
1/4 teaspoon almond flavoring
5 to 10 teaspoons 2 percent milk
3/4 teaspoon powdered cocoa
2 drops yellow food coloring
1-12 ounce jar cherry jam

Directions:
Whisk the flour, baking soda and salt in a bowl until it is well combined and set aside.

Cream the butter and sugar in the mixer until light and fluffy. Add the egg and vanilla and mix in well. Gradually add the flour mixture to butter mixture until it is all incorporated. Scoop the dough out onto a lightly floured surface and shape in 2 – 6 inch long rolls. Wrap each roll with plastic and refrigerate at least 1 hour.

Preheat your oven to 375 degrees F and line cookie sheets with parchment paper.

Cut the logs into 3/8 inch slices and place on the baking sheets about 2 inches apart. Bake for 8 to 10 minutes or until light brown. Cool completely on wire racks.

Cream the butter, confectiones' sugar, 1 teaspoon vanilla and 1/4 teaspoon almond flavoring in the mixer. Add the cocoa and yellow food coloring and mix in well. Add enough of the milk to make it easy to pipe the mixture through a pastry bag. Fill the pastry bag with the frosting. Spread a little cherry jam on each slice to 1/4 inch of the edge and pipe lines like lattice work over top each cookie. You can even pipe an edge around the top of the cookie if you would like.

CARAMEL COOKIE CUPS

These are decadently sweet. You use an unwrapped caramel in each cookie that is surrounded by a flaky crust covered with a frosting. This recipe makes 48 cookies.

Ingredients:
1 cup softened butter
6 ounces softened cream cheese
2 cups all-purpose flour
1*14 ounce package caramels in individual wrapping
1/2 cup evaporated milk
1/2 cup granulated sugar
1 cup shortening
1/3 cup more of evaporated milk
1 teaspoon vanilla

Directions:
Preheat your oven to 350 degrees F.

In your mixer combine the butter and cream cheese until creamy. Add the flour gradually until it is well blended. You should have a nice soft dough. Pinch off 48 pieces of equal size (about a teaspoonful) and press into mini tassie pans. These look like cupcake pans but the individual cakes are much smaller. They are also used to make pecan tarts. Press so they cover the bottom and come up to the top of the little indentations. Bake for 15 minutes or until they are light brown. Cool in the pans. These do not have to be totally cool to continue and can be warm.

Melt the caramels (all of them) and 1/2 cup evaporated milk in a microwave safe dish in the microwave. Put it in a few minutes at a time and stir after each session. Once the caramels are creamy spoon the caramel filling into each of the little cups.

To make the frosting, beat in the mixer the sugar, 1/3 cup evaporated milk, shortening and vanilla until it is light and creamy. Frost each cookie over top the caramel.

Variation: Sprinkle the top of the cookies with chopped pecans or mini-chocolate chips. Instead of using caramels, use chocolate caramels for a different flavor.

PECAN TASSIE COOKIES

These cookies are like pecan pie with a cream cheese crust. They are absolutely delicious. The recipe makes about 24 tiny pie-like cookies.

Ingredients:
1/2 cup softened butter
1-3 ounce package of softened cream cheese
1 cup all-purpose flour
Filling:
1 egg beaten
3/4 cup brown sugar packed tight
1 tablespoon melted butter
1/2 cup chopped pecans

To make the dough, beat the butter and cream cheese in your mixer until it is light and fluffy. Gradually add the flour until it makes a soft dough. Wrap the dough in plastic wrap and put it in the refrigerator for at least 1 hour.

Preheat the oven to 325 degrees F. Take the dough out and shape into 24 little balls and put the balls in an ungreased tassie pan in each compartment. Press the dough into the bottom and up the sides.

In your mixer bowl beat the egg and add the brown sugar and melted butter to cream the mixture well. Remove from the mixer and hand stir in the pecans. Fill the dough cups equally with the pecan mixture and bake for 30 minutes or until the dough edges become brown and the centers are firm. Cool in the pans for about 15 to 20 minutes and pop out onto wire racks to cool all the way.

LEMON CURT TART COOKIES

These cookies are lemony good and are made similarly to the pecan cookies above. In fact, use the same dough recipe and prepare pans as done above. However, you cook the shells before adding the lemon curd in this recipe. Just fill the cups of the pan with the dough and push down and up the sides and bake in a preheated 400 degree F oven for 10 to 12 minutes or until the crusts get lightly browned. Cool in pan and start the filling. Only put the filling in when the shells are completely cool or they will get very soggy.

Ingredients for Filling:
3 beaten eggs
1 – 1/4 cup granulated sugar
1/3 cup lemon juice
1/4 cup butter
3/4 teaspoon lemon zest

Combine the beaten eggs, sugar, lemon juice and butter in a medium sauce pan and heat over medium heat. Constantly stir and cook turning down if the mixture starts to bubble too much. It should start to thicken and be thick and done in about 15 minutes. Stir in the lemon zest and let cool. Once the filling is cool, chill in the refrigerator about 1 hour. Spoon equally into the finished shells. These must be kept cool so store in an airtight container in the refrigerator.

Variation: Add some mini chocolate chips to the filling for a sweet and sour flavor. Sprinkle crushed almonds over the top.

WHOOPIE PIE COOKIES

These cookies are chocolate sandwich cookies that are cake-like filled with a creamy filling. Everyone loves them. This recipe only makes 6, but they are pretty big.

Ingredients:
2 cups all-purpose flour
5 tablespoons unsweetened cocoa powder
1/4 teaspoon salt
1 teaspoon baking soda
1/2 cup shortening
1 cup granulated sugar
2 egg yolks (save the whites for the filling)
1 cup milk
1 teaspoon vanilla
Filling
3/4 cup shortening
2 cups confectioners' sugar
2 egg whites
1 pinch of salt
1 teaspoon of vanilla

Directions:
Preheat your oven to 350 degrees F and cover baking sheets with parchment paper sprayed with non stick spray.

Whisk together the flour, cocoa powder, salt and baking soda. Set aside until later. Cream the 1/2 cup shortening and granulated sugar until light and fluffy. Add the egg yolks and beat in. Gradually add the flour mixture to the shortening mixture alternately with the milk until all are combined making a soft dough. Add the vanilla and mix in well.

Scoop out dough with a large spoon and drop onto the cookie sheets about 1 inch apart. Bake for 10 to 15 minutes and remove to a cooling rack to cool. Do not proceed until the cookies are completely cool.

In your mixer bowl beat the 3/4 cup shortening with the confectioners' sugar until well mixed. Add the egg whites, salt and vanilla and beat well making a creamy frosting. Spread the flat side of one of the cookie with the filling and top with another cookie. Wrap these in wax paper and twist at both ends.

Variation: Add 1/2 cup mini chocolate chips hand stirred into the frosting.

LADYLOCKS OR CLOTHES PIN COOKIES

Sometimes these are called Lady Locks because they look like spiral curls, but they are actually baked on clean clothespins. The dough is very delicate, almost like puff pastry and the filling is sweet and creamy. This recipe makes 18 cookies. Use new clothespins and wrap them with foil and spray with non-stick spray or cut 5/8 inch wooden dowels that are 4 inches long. Use an insulated cookie sheet if you possibly can.

Ingredients:
1 pound softened butter
3 cups all-purpose flour
2 tablespoons granulated sugar
2 egg yolks
1-1/4 cups ice water
Filling
1 cup milk
1/2 cup all-purpose flour
1-1/2 cups shortening
8 cups confectioners' sugar
1-7 ounce container of marshmallow cream
1 teaspoon vanilla

Directions:
In a large bowl place 1/4 cup of the softened butter, flour, granulated sugar, egg yolks and water. Use a pastry blender to cut in like pie dough. You might have to use your hands at the end, but do this sparingly. (Use a food processor if you have one) Roll the dough into a ball, cover in plastic wrap and refrigerate for 1 hour.

Roll all the dough out into a rectangle on a floured board. Spread the surface with 1/4 cup more of the butter. Fold the dough over the butter by taking one edge and folding it to the middle and taking the opposite edge and folding it over again. Refrigerate 1 hour take it out, roll it, spread and fold until all the butter is used up. This will be four times. After the last time cut the dough into fourths and wrap each quarter separately in plastic wrap. Chill another hour.

Preheat the oven to 400 degrees F.

Take out one quarter and let it stand at room temperature so that it softens enough to be rolled. This will take about 15 minutes or so. Flour a board and roll out the dough. Cut into 1/2 inch wide and 4.5 inch long strips. Wrap these strips loosely on the clothespin so that non of the clothespin shows underneath. Pinch the ends so they don't fall off. Place them on an ungreased baking sheet covered with parchment paper and bake for 12 to 15 minutes or until light brown. Let cool about 10 minutes. Cover hands with a clean towel and carefully slide each cookie off the clothespin. They break very easily so be very careful. Let cool on cooling racks completely.

To make the filling use a medium saucepan over medium heat and cook the 1 cup milk and 1/2 cup flour until it gets thick. Stir constantly so it doesn't stick to the bottom of the pan. Let this cool

In the mixer cream the shortening, confectioners' sugar, marshmallow cream and the vanilla. Add the cooled cooked mixture to the creamed mixture and beat until it is very creamy and fluffy. Fill a pastry bag with a large tip with the filling and pipe into the pastry. Dust with confectioners' sugar and store in air tight containers.

Chapter 6: No Bake Cookies that Taste Great

The words "No Bake" might have a different connotation to some people than to others. "No Bake" does not mean that the ingredients do not have to go through some sort of process that involves heat. It does mean that the cookies do not have to cook in the oven. Some ingredients are actually put in a pan over the stove to cook. Therefore, it is not always safe for a child to make no bake cookies by him or herself. An adult should be present in order to cook the ingredients on the stove or in the microwave so there is no chance of being burned.

The accepted history of no bake cookies sounds a little fishy to me. Apparently, the cookies were invented by a poor man who was not able to feed his family. He was carrying a bag of oats and tripped over a log by the fire where his wife was melting chocolate to make candy. I don't know about you, but if I didn't have enough food to feed my family, it would be very unlikely I would have chocolate to melt over a fire.

No matter where they came from, no bake cookies are fun to make and delicious to eat. In the Appalachians the common no bake made from chocolate and oats are called preacher cookies. The reason they had this name was because when the people saw the preacher coming to visit on horseback at the bottom of the mountain, they had enough time to make no bake cookies and have them cooled for when he got there. I'm still trying to figure out how the poor people in the Appalachians were able to have that chocolate on hand whenever they needed it.

Today we can make no bake cookies out of many things and they have different flavors and textures. Here is a tip about boiling the ingredients for the cookies. Take a stick of butter that is partial softened and wipe the rim of the saucepan with a wide swipe. Even when in a rolling boil, the ingredients will not go beyond that line of butter and you will prevent spill overs.

CHOCOLATE BUTTERSCOTCH NO BAKE COOKIES

These cookies are made from chocolate chips, butterscotch chips and rice cereal. The recipe makes 48 bars and takes only about 45 minutes to get ready and eat.

Ingredients:
1 cup semi-sweet chocolate chips
1 cup butterscotch chips
1 cup granulated sugar
1 cup light corn syrup
1 cup smooth peanut butter
6 cups rice cereal

Directions:

Place both types of chips in a glass bowl that is microwave safe. Melt them by microwaving on high for one minute at a time stirring after each minute until the chips are melted and creamy.

Meanwhile, place the granulated sugar and corn syrup in a large, heavy sauce pan and heat over medium heat. Let the mixture come to a rolling bowl in the middle and remove from the heat. Add the peanut butter and stir in well. Mix in the rice cereal making sure it is all coated. Press this mixture into a buttered 9 by 13 inch pan and spread the chocolate chip and butterscotch chip mixture over top. Place in the refrigerator for about 1 hour and cut into bars.

Variation: Use crunchy peanut butter for a crunchier texture.

CHOCOLATE OATMEAL NO BAKE COOKIES WITH CRUNCHY PEANUT BUTTER

These are pretty close to the preacher cookies talked about in the first paragraphs of this chapter. The recipe makes 30 cookies and it only takes about an hour to make them.

Ingredients:
3 cups granulated sugar
3 tablespoons unsweetened cocoa powder
1/2 cup milk
1/2 cup butter
3 tablespoons crunchy peanut butter
1 teaspoon vanilla
3 cups old fashion rolled oats (do not use quick oats or steel cut oats)

Directions:
Place the sugar, cocoa powder, milk, butter and peanut butter in a large sauce pan. Stir constantly while brining to a boil over medium heat. Once it comes to a rolling boil, continue to boil for 1-1/2 minutes without stirring at all. Remove the pan from heat and stir in the vanilla then the rolled oats. Drop by teaspoonfuls onto a cookie sheet that has been covered with wax paper. Let cool and store in an airtight container.

Variation: Add some candy coated chocolate candy to the mix for color.

PEANUT BUTTER NO BAKE BARS

These bring the flavor of peanut butter, graham crackers and chocolate together in a lovely no bake bar. They honestly taste like a peanut butter cup. The recipe makes 12 bars or squares and takes about 1 hour and a half to make and cool enough to cut.

Ingredients:
1 cup butter or margarine that has been melted

2 cups graham cracker crumbs
2 cups confectioners' sugar
1 cup smooth peanut butter
1 -1/2 cups semi sweet chocolate chips
4 tablespoons more of the peanut butter

Directions:
Place the butter, graham cracker crumbs, confectioners' sugar and the 1 cup peanut butter in a bowl and mix by hand until it is well combined. Press this mixture into the bottom of a 9 by 13 pan that is ungreased.

Place the chocolate chips and the 4 tablespoons of peanut butter in a microwave safe bowl and microwave on high for one minute at a time stirring after each minute until the mixture becomes melted and creamy. Spread this over the combination in the 9 by 13 inch pan. Place the pan in the refrigerator for 1 your and cut into squares.

Variation: Sprinkle the top of the pan with Peanut Butter flavored coated chocolate candy before you put the pan in the refrigerator.

BUCKEYES

These cookies do resemble the Buckeye, a nut like object that comes from the buckeye tree that is round and has 1/4 of the one end a light tan and the rest a dark chestnut brown. Buckeyes are very popular in Ohio as it is the State Tree and the Buckeyes are the name of Ohio State's Football team. These cookie do resemble buckeyes and this recipe makes 30 of them.

Ingredients:
1 cup softened butter
1-1/2 cups smooth peanut butter
6 cups confectioners' sugar
1/2 teaspoon vanilla
4 cups semi-sweet chocolate chips

Directions:
Place the butter, peanut butter, confectioners' sugar and vanilla in a large bowl and mix well. You can do this with a mixer or with a pastry cutter. The dough is dry and slightly crumbly but will press into a form. Roll the dough into 1 inch balls and place them on a cookie sheet that has been lined with wax paper.

Poke a toothpick into the top of each ball and leave them there. Place the cookie sheets in the refrigerator to chill the dough for about 30 minutes

Right before removing from the refrigerator, melt the chocolate chips in a microwave safe bowl, microwaving on high for 1 minute at a time and stirring after each minute until the chips are melted and creamy.

Take the chilled peanut butter balls by the toothpick and swirl it in the melted chocolate keeping the very top part where the toothpick is inserted showing. Put the chocolate covered cookies back on the cookie sheet and put back in the refrigerator for about 20 minutes. Remove the toothpicks and serve or place in an airtight container. Always store uneaten cookies in the refrigerator.

IRISH POTATO COOKIES

This is an old recipe that only look like potatoes. You don't use potatoes to make them. Instead they are made with coconut and cream cheese. This recipe makes about 60 of the little potatoes.

Ingredients:
1/2 package (8 ounces) softened cream cheese
1/4 cup softened butter
1 teaspoon vanilla
4 cups confectioners' sugar
2-1/2 cups flaked coconut
1 tablespoon ground cinnamon

Directions:
Beat the cream cheese and butter together in a mixer bowl until it is smooth and creamy. Add the vanilla and add the confectioners' sugar gradually until it is all mixed in. Remove from the mixer and mix in the coconut by hand. Roll the dough into little potato shapes. Place the cinnamon in a small bowl and roll each potato cookie in the cinnamon and place it on a cookie sheet covered with wax paper. Chill in the refrigerator for about 1 hour.

Variation: If the cinnamon is too strong for you, add 1/2 tablespoon granulated sugar to the mixture to tone it down.

NO BAKE RUM BALLS

The combination of the rum and chocolate make for a nice combination. Just be aware you are using uncooked rum that has the alcohol in them. Avoid letting children sample these cookies and only take them to appropriate types of parties. You also may want to put a sign on them saying they do contain alcohol so no one that should not have it, gets any. You can make them rum free and this is in the variation section. This recipe makes 2 dozen cookies.

Ingredients:
1-1/2 cup chopped nuts
3/4 cup confectioners' sugar
1-12 ounce package of vanilla wafers crushed fine in a food processor
1/4 cup cocoa
3 tablespoons light corn syrup

1-1/2 cup light rum
1/8 cup more of confectioners' sugar

Directions:
Place the nuts, 3/4 cup confectioners' sugar, vanilla wafers and cocoa in a large bowl and whisk with a wire whisk to combine well. Add the corn syrup and rum and mix with a spoon until it is all well combined. The dough should stick together to make 1 inch balls. Roll each ball in a bowl with the 1/8 cup confectioners' sugar in it and place in an airtight container about 2 to 3 days before serving. This lets the rum age and develop the most flavor it can. Roll them in confectioners' sugar again, right before serving

Variation: To make a non-alcoholic cookie Use 1/2 cup orange juice and 1 teaspoon of grated orange zest instead of the rum.

To make bourbon balls, use pecans instead of just chopped nuts and use 3/4 cup bourbon instead of rum.

NO BAKE DATE AND COCONUT BALLS

This recipe makes 2 dozen cookies that are super simple to make. If you like coconut, you will love these and you can dye the coconut with food coloring to make them colorful.

Ingredients:
1 cup granulated sugar
1 cup chopped dates
2 eggs that have been beaten
1 tablespoon butter
1 teaspoon vanilla
3 cups rice cereal
1 cup flaked coconut

Directions:
Place the sugar, dates and beaten eggs in a saucepan and heat over medium heat until it comes to a boil. Stir occasionally and let boil for a full 5 minutes. Don't let any of the mixture stick to the bottom of the pan and burn. Remove the pan from heat and add the butter and vanilla. Let it cool slightly

Mix this mixture with the rice cereal. You may have to use your hands so make sure the dough is not too hot. Butter your hands to keep it from sticking. Place the coconut in a bowl. Roll dough into 1 inch balls and roll in coconut. Store in an airtight container until serving.

Variation: Use 1 teaspoon of orange extract instead of vanilla for a citrus flavor.

NO BAKE ORANGE BALLS

These cookies have the fresh flavor of orange and are served chilled. They are great for a summer party when you need something cool to eat. This recipe makes 36 cookies.

Ingredients:
4 cups confectioners' sugar
1/2 cup softened butter
1-6 ounce can frozen orange juice that has been thawed
1-12 ounce package of vanilla wafers
1 cup flaked coconut

Directions:
Place the sugar, butter and orange juice in a large bowl. Crush the vanilla wafers in a food processor and add. Mix well to make a gooey dough. Shape dough into 1 inch balls. Place coconut in a small bowl and roll each ball in it. Store cookies in an airtight container that has been placed in the refrigerator at least 1 hour before serving. Serve cold.

Variation: Instead of rolling in coconut, roll the cookies in chopped pecans.

HEALTHY NO BAKE GRANOLA BARS

These bars contain flaxseed that is easily found at health food stores. Flaxseed is good for the body because it is full of Omega-3 Fatty Acids and Fiber. Flaxseed is thought to fight cancer, heart disease and lung disease as well. It is combined with all kinds of goodies to make this delicious granola cookie bar. This recipe makes 12 bars.

Ingredients:
1-1/4 cups crunchy style peanut butter
3/4 cup honey
3/4 cup dried cranberries
1/4 cup sliced almonds
1/2 cup chocolate chips
1 cup ground flaxseed
2 cups rolled oats

Directions:
In a large bowl, mix all the above ingredients making sure everything is coated with the peanut butter and honey. Pour the ingredients into a 9 by 11 inch baking dish and use the back of a wooden spoon or spatula to press it into the dish and flatten it out. Refrigerate for at least 1 hour and take it cutting it into 12 bars. Wrap each of the bars in plastic wrap.

Variation: Use dried apricots or raisins instead of cranberries.

NO BAKE HAYSTACK COOKIES

These cookies really do look like little haystacks and they are crunchy under the peanut butter and butterscotch because of the peanuts and chow mein noodles that make them look like haystacks. This recipe makes 12 haystack cookies

Ingredients:
1/2 cup smooth peanut butter
1 cup butterscotch chips
1/2 cup salted peanuts
2 cups chow mein noodles

Directions:
Place the peanut butter and butterscotch chops in a microwave safe bowl and stir them around to mix them up a bit. Place the bowl in the microwave and heat on high for 1.5 minutes. Stir the contents and put it back in, one minute on high at a time, until it is all melted and thick.

Stir the peanuts and the chow mein noodles in. Use a fork to scoop out about a teaspoonful and set it on wax paper. Let cool to room temperature until they are set and do not fall apart. Store in an airtight container.

Variation: Make chocolate haystacks by using chocolate chips instead of butterscotch chips

TOASTY OAT CEREAL COOKIE BARS

This recipe makes about 15 bar cookies and they are made out of toasted "O" shaped breakfast cereal. There is honey in the recipe, so avoid giving this to little kids under 2 years old.

Ingredients:
1/2 cup honey
1/2 cup granulated sugar
1/2 cup smooth peanut butter
1 cup salted peanuts
3 cups toasted oat cereal

Directions:
Place the honey and granulated sugar in a heavy, large saucepan and cook over medium heat, stirring constantly. Bring to a boil and remove from heat. Add the peanut butter and stir in to melt. Once it is melted stir in the peanuts and oat cereal and mix well.

Spray a 9 by 13 inch pan with non-stick spray and press the mixture in flattening it out with the back of a spoon. Let it cool and cut into bars once it becomes firm. Store in an airtight container.

Variation: Omit the peanuts if someone in the family has a peanut allergy. If you want to take it up a notch use salted cashews instead of peanuts.

PEANUT BUTTER COCONUT NO BAKE BARS

This recipe also contains honey, so be careful who you give them to. The recipe makes about 24 peanutty flavored bars that are very hard to resist.

Ingredients:
16 graham crackers
2/3 cup honey
1/2 cup non-fat dry milk
1 cup crunch peanut butter
1 cup flaked coconut

Directions:
Place the graham crackers between two pieces of wax paper and crush with a rolling pin, or you can just whirl them around in a food processor until crumbs. Place the crackers, honey, dry milk, and peanut butter in a large bowl and mix well by hand.

Place the coconut in a small bowl. Scoop out teaspoonfuls of the dough and roll it into 1 inch balls. Roll them in the coconut before setting on a wax paper covered cookie sheet. Store in an airtight container until serving.

Variation: Use Nutella instead of peanut butter for a different flavor.

S'MORES YOU MAKE INDOORS

Everyone likes s'mores made with graham crackers, marshmallows, and chocolate bars. This version is made indoors and you can have them any time. This recipe makes 16 no bake cookies. They absolutely must be stored in an airtight container but they do not need to be refrigerated unless it is very hot and muggy in the house.

Ingredients:
6 cup mini marshmallows
3 tablespoons margarine or butter
1/4 cup light corn syrup
1-1/2 cups milk chocolate chips
4 cups honey graham flavored cereal

Directions:
Place the marshmallows, margarine or butter and corn syrup in a large, heavy saucepan and heat over medium heat stirring constantly until it is all melted. Stir until smooth. Add the chocolate chips and keep stirring until they are melted.

Spray a 9 by 13 inch baking dish with non-stick spray and pour the honey graham cereal in. Pour the marshmallow mixture over top and stir it well so that it coats all the cereal. Press with the back of a spoon into the pan so it is firm. Cool and cut into squares.

Chapter 7: Special Occasion Cookies

Special occasion cookies might include holiday recipes or Christmas Cookies and maybe a few wedding type cookies. These are the cookies you want to make to impress people, or they might become a tradition in your household. Many of the cookies that have been in the other chapters can be made into Christmas or other holiday cookies. Rum and Bourbon balls are a tradition at Christmas and you can also deck the cookie with holiday motifs. Chocolate chip bars with a little red and green sugar sprinkled on top make a great holiday treat. Make regular sugar cookies and cut them in shapes for the holidays decorating with royal icing (this recipe is included right after the Gingerbread People recipe).

GINGERBREAD PEOPLE

Who can even think of Christmas without some gingerbread people. Cookie cutters for both men and women come in all shapes and sizes. You can make a batch putting a hole at the top, bake and decorate them, cover with plastic wrap to keep them fresh and insert a ribbon or wire through the hole to hang the cookie on the tree. This recipe makes about 30 cookies using a smaller cookie cutter.

Ingredients:
2 cups all-purpose flour
1/4 teaspoon salt
1/2 teaspoon baking soda
1/2 teaspoon baking powder
1/2 teaspoon ground cinnamon
1/2 teaspoon ground cloves
1/2 teaspoon ground ginger
1/2 teaspoon ground nutmeg
1/2 cup margarine (you can use shortening – I prefer butter flavored)
1/2 cup sugar
1/2 cup molasses
1 egg yolk

Directions:
Mix together the flour, salt, baking soda, baking powder, cinnamon, cloves, ginger and nutmeg in a large bowl with a wire whisk. Place the margarine or shortening in a mixer bowl and add the sugar. Cream on high until light and fluffy. Pour in the molasses while the mixture is beating on medium low and also add the egg yolk. Mix well and gradually start adding the flour mixture beating well after each addition. Form the dough in a ball, wrap in plastic wrap and chill in the refrigerator for at least 1 hour.

Preheat your oven to 35 degrees F and prepare baking sheets with parchment paper on top.

Roll the dough out with a rolling pin on a floured surface to about 1/4 inch thick. Use cookie cutters to cut gingerbread people out and place 2 inch apart on prepared cookie sheets.

Bake 8 to 10 minutes until the cookie is firm. They will be brown, so it is hard to tell if they are done by color. Cool on cookie sheets for 10 minutes and remove to cooling racks. Frost when totally cool

ROYAL ICING

You used to use egg whites to make royal icing, but since that can cause food poisoning, you use meringue powder. All that is is cooked and dehydrated egg whites with a few other things added in. Royal icing is hard and creates a crust, but it is still good and sweet to the taste. You can color it any color with food coloring. I prefer the solid food coloring rather than drops because the colors are more vivid.

Ingredients:
4 cups confectioners' sugar
3 tablespoons meringue powder
6 tablespoons water

Directions:
Place all the ingredients in your mixer bowl and start beating on low speed for 7 to 10 minutes. The icing should form stiff peaks. Place some of the icing in separate glass bowls and add food coloring. Mix in by hand just to blend. To much stirring can make the icing fall. This icing dries out quickly so always cover it with a clean, damp kitchen towel to keep moist while you are frosting the cookies.

Add raisins for eyes, red hots or jelly beans for buttons, snow caps for hair and any other candy for decoration. It will stick on the cookie with a little dollop of royal icing underneath.

PFEFFERNUSSE COOKIES

These are German cookies with a gingerbread flavor and yes, there is pepper in them. They have a very strong flavor, so little children might not like them much, but adults adore them. Many people put candied cherries or pineapple in them, but this recipe does not. You can add the finely chopped candied fruit if you would like. I like them better without it. This recipe makes about 18 balls.

Ingredients:
1/4 cup honey
1/4 cup shortening
1/2 cup dark molasses
1/4 cup softened butter or margarine

1 teaspoon vanilla extract
2 eggs
3/4 cup granulated sugar
1/2 cup brown sugar packed tight
4 cups all-purpose flour
1-1/2 teaspoon baking soda
1 teaspoon ground cloves
1 teaspoon ground ginger
1 teaspoon ground nutmeg
1-1/2 teaspoons ground cardamom
2 teaspoons ground cinnamon
1 teaspoon ground black pepper
1/4 teaspoon salt
1 cup confectioners' sugar

Place the honey, shortening, molasses and butter in a large saucepan and heat over medium. Stir constantly and cook until it becomes creamy. Add the vanilla extract. Remove from the heat and cool to room temperature. Stir in the eggs by hand until they are well mixed in.

Place the flour, both sugars, baking soda, all the spices, pepper and salt in a large bowl. Pour in the honey and molasses mixture and mix by hand with a rubber spatula until it is well combined. This will take some muscle. Use a wooden spoon if you have to or just use your hands to get it all well combined. Cover the bowl with plastic wrap and chill in the refrigerator for 2 hours.

Preheat the oven to 325 degrees and cover cookie sheets with parchment paper. Scoop out the dough and roll into balls about the size of a large acorn. Place on the baking sheets about 1 inch apart and bake for 10 to 15 minutes. Remove to a cooling rack to cool. Place the confectioners' sugar in a bowl and roll each ball in it before putting in an air tight container.

Variation: If you would like to add more flavor (like they don't have enough already) do not add the vanilla and add 1 teaspoon of anise flavoring. This is what the old recipe included, but I find them to be a little too spicy for me with the anise. If you wish to add the chopped candied fruit, add about 1/2 to 3/4 cup while mixing everything together.

CHOCOLATE CRINKLES OR KRINGLES

These delicious chocolate cookies crack on the top after being rolled in confectioners' sugar and make a cracked look on top that looks crinkly. To make them Christmasy, some people call them kringles (as in Kris Kringle) instead. This recipe makes about 72 servings. The cookies can be frozen.

Ingredients:
2 cups all-purpose flour

2 teaspoons baking powder
1/4 teaspoon salt
1/2 cup vegetable oil
1 cup unsweetened cocoa powder
2 cups granulated sugar
4 eggs
1-1/2 teaspoons vanilla
1/2 cup confectioners' sugar

Directions:
Preheat your oven to 350 degrees and cover cookie sheets with parchment paper.

Whisk together the flour, baking powder and salt in a bowl and set aside. In your mixer bowl, beat the oil, cocoa powder and sugar until it is creamed well. Add the eggs and vanilla and beat well. Gradually add the flour mixture until it is all mixed in. The dough will be soft.

Scoop out teaspoonfuls of the dough and roll into balls. Roll each ball in confectioners' sugar before placing about 1 inch apart on the cookie sheets. Bake 10 to 12 minutes. Remove from oven and let sit on cookie sheets about 2 to 5 minutes before removing to a wire rack. They should be very crinkled.

Variation: Instead of a whole cup of cocoa powder, make espresso crinkles by substituting 3/4 cup cocoa and 1/4 cup espresso powder.

PEANUT BUTTER BLOSSOMS

These cookies do look like flower blossoms. They are a peanut butter cookie with a candy kiss situated right in the center. This recipe makes 84 cookies, but don't worry, they freeze and they will probably be eaten up right away.

Ingredients:
3-1/2 cups all-purpose flour
2 teaspoons baking soda
1/2 teaspoon salt
1 cup shortening
1 cup smooth peanut butter
1 cup brown sugar packed tight
1 cup granulated sugar
2 eggs
1/4 cup milk
1-1/2 teaspoon vanilla
1/2 cup more granulated sugar
2-9 ounce packages of milk chocolate kisses all unwrapped

Directions:

Preheat the oven to 375 degrees and cover cookies sheets with parchment paper sprayed with a little non-stick spray.

Whisk the flour, baking soda and salt in a large bowl until well combined and set aside. Place the shortening, peanut butter, brown sugar and 1 cup granulated sugar in the mixer bowl and cream until smooth. Add the eggs, one at a time mixing in well and then add the milk and vanilla. Gradually add the flour mixture to the shortening mixture until it is all well combined.
Scoop out tablespoons of the dough and roll into balls. Roll these balls in the 1/2 cup granulated sugar placed in a small bowl and place 2 inches apart on the cookie sheets.

Bake 10 to 12 minutes or until lightly brown and puffy. Remove from the oven and immediately press the kiss into the center of the cookie. Don't press too hard to come all the way through to the cookie sheet. Let the cookies sit on the cookie sheet a full 10 minutes and remove to wire cooling racks.

SPRITZ COOKIES

To make these cookies you will need a cookie press. You put the dough in the tube of the press and place a mold like disk at the bottom. When you press the cookie dough out, it comes out in a shape. You can make little flower-like shapes that resemble snowflakes or a Christmas tree shape. If you use the tree shape, color the dough green and top with little candy sprinkles before baking. You can even make sandwich cookies from Spritz cookies by placing frosting in between two snowflake-like cookies. This recipe makes about 72 cookies depending on the shape. Spritz cookies freeze well with or without the frosting.

Ingredients:
5 cups all-purpose flour
1/2 teaspoon salt
2 cups butter (You can use shortening, but sometimes the cookies are not stiff enough unless you use butter)
2-1/2 cups confectioners' sugar
2 eggs
1 teaspoon almond extract
1 teaspoon vanilla

Directions:
Preheat you oven to 400 degrees and cover cookie sheets with parchment paper.

Whisk together the flour and the salt and set the bowl aside. Place the butter and confectioners' sugar in your mixer bowl and beat on low until the mixture starts to cream. Beat in the eggs, almond extract and vanilla and beat well. Gradually add the flour mixture to the shortening mixture until it is all combined.

Fill the cookie press and press cookies on the parchment covered cookie sheets about 1 inch apart. You might want to practice. Press into the cookie sheet when pressing and stop pressing and lift off. It does take some practice.

Bake for 6 to 8 minutes or until golden brown. The green trees will get brown around the edges. Don't let them get too brown. Remove to cooling racks immediately. Cool before adding frosting in the middle of two cookies.

JAM THUMBPRINTS

This is a traditional holiday cookie made with jam and coated with nuts. The recipe makes about 24 servings. These do not freeze well because the jam will make them a little soggy. Use any kind of jam you wish; you don't have to stick to just one kind for this whole batch.

Ingredients:
2 cups all-purpose flour
1/2 teaspoon salt
1 cup softened butter
1/2 cup brown sugar packed tight
2 eggs (separated – keep the yolks for the dough and the whites for later)
1 teaspoon vanilla
1/2 cup finely chopped walnuts
1-1/2 cup jam

Directions:
Preheat oven to 300 degrees and cover cookie sheets with parchment paper sprayed lightly with non-stick spray.

Whisk the flour and salt in a bowl and set aside. Place the butter and brown sugar in a mixer bowl and cream until smooth. Add the egg yolks only and vanilla and beat in. Gradually add the flour mixture to the butter mixture until it is well combined.

Have ready the egg whites saved from the dough. Scoop out teaspoonfuls of the dough and roll into balls. Roll each ball in the egg whites then in the nuts and place on the cookie sheets about 2 inches from each other and bake for 5 minutes. Remove the cookies from the oven and dent each cookie with a thumb. They will be hot. You can use a the back of a baby spoon so you don't burn your fingers. Spoon the jam into the dents and replace in the oven and bake 6 more minutes or until brown. Immediately remove to cooling racks.

Variation: If you don't like nuts, don't use them and make them plain thumb prints.

VIENNESE HAZELNUT CRESCENTS

These cookies are light and flaky with a flavor of hazelnuts. The recipe makes about 48 cookies and they freeze reasonably well although better when fresh.

Ingredients:
2 cups all-purpose flour
1/8 teaspoon salt
1 cup ground hazelnuts
1 cup butter (only use butter)
1/2 cup confectioners' sugar
1 teaspoon vanilla
2 cups more confectioners' sugar
1 vanilla bean

Whisk together the flour, salt and ground nuts in a large bowl and set aside. Place the butter and 1/2 cup confectioners' sugar in a mixer bowl and beat until creamed. Add the vanilla. Gradually add the flour until the mixer has a hard time. You will then proceed mixing with your hands. Shape into a ball, place in plastic wrap and put in refrigerator for at least 1 hour.

Preheat the oven to 375 degrees and cover cookie sheets with parchment paper.

Place the 2 cups confectioners' sugar into a bowl. Cut the vanilla bean pod lengthwise and separate. Scrape out the little black seeds on both sides and add to the confectioners' sugar. Mix in well and set aside.

Scoop out dough by the teaspoonful and shape into a ball, then roll into a 3 inch long roll and set on cookies sheets 2 inches apart. Bend the roll into a crescent shape.

Bake for 10 to 12 minutes until they are set, but do not let them brown. Remove from the oven and let set for 2 to 3 minutes. Scoop off cookie sheets and into the bowl with the confectioners' sugar and vanilla bean. Roll well and set on a sheet of aluminum foil to cool. Store in an airtight container.

Variation: Use ground almonds instead of hazelnuts.

NOELS

This is a holiday bar cookie that makes about 18 bars filled with walnuts.

Ingredients:
5 tablespoons all-purpose flour
1/8 teaspoon baking soda
1/8 teaspoon salt
2 tablespoons butter
1 cup brown sugar packed tight
2 beaten eggs

1 teaspoon vanilla
1 cup chopped walnuts
1/4 cup confectioners' sugar

Directions:
Preheat the oven to 350 degrees.

Whisk together the flour, baking soda and salt in a large bowl and set aside. Place the butter in a 7 by 11 inch baking pan. Place in the oven just long enough for it to melt and tip it so that the butter coats the inside of the pan.

Place the brown sugar, eggs and vanilla in a mixer bowl and beat until creamy. Add the flour mixture gradually until it is well combined. Hand stir in the walnuts and pour into the pan over the butter. Bake for 20 minutes or until edges begin to brown. Cool and dust with the confectioners' sugar. Cut into bars.

RUSSIAN TEA COOKIES

This cookie has a dough that was very common around the middle ages in many different areas including England and Russia. It was made from butter, flour, sugar and nuts. Russian tea cookies are usually made with walnuts, almonds or hazelnuts while Mexican tea cookies are made with pecans. These also look like snowballs, so they made them selves a part of Christmas festivities in many families. This recipe makes about 36 cookies and should be stored in an air tight container.

Ingredients:
2 cups all-purpose flour
6 tablespoons confectioners' sugar
1 cup softened butter
1 teaspoon vanilla
1 cup chopped walnuts, almonds or hazelnuts
1/3 cup more of confectioners' sugar

Directions:
Preheat your oven to 350 degrees and cover cookie sheets with parchment paper.

Whisk together the flour and 6 tablespoons of confectioners' sugar in a large bowl and set aside. Place the butter in a mixer bowl and cream along with the vanilla. Add the flour mixture adding gradually to the butter mixture until just combined. Hand mix in the nuts that have been chopped very fine. Roll the dough into 1 inch balls and put them on the paper covered cookie sheets about 1 inch apart.

Bake for 10 to 12 minutes and remove to cooling racks when done. Once the cookie is cool, place the remaining 1/3 cup confectioners' sugar in a bowl and roll each cookie in it to cover it well.

SPICY CINNAMON STAR COOKIES

The German for these cookies is "Zimi Sterne" and there is no flour in them. You use ground almonds and they are gluten-free because of that. They are also pretty pricey and are used at special occasions. This recipe makes about 18 to 20 cookies depending on the size of the cookie cutter used.

Ingredients:
2 egg whites
1/8 teaspoon salt
2-1/2 cups of confectioners' sugar
2-2/3 cups ground almonds
1 tablespoon ground cinnamon
1 teaspoon lemon zest
1-3/4 teaspoons lemon juice

Directions:
Preheat the oven to 325 degrees and cover cookie sheets with parchment paper.

Place the egg whites in the mixture with the salt and beat until soft peaks come up. Gradually add the confectioners' sugar until the contents of the bowl are very stiff. Scoop out 1/3 cup of the this mixture and set aside.

Place the almonds, cinnamon and lemon zest in a bowl and whisk to combine well. Add this to the egg mixture in the bowl by folding it in by hand very carefully.

Roll the dough on a surface that has been primed with more confectioners' sugar. Roll out to 1/4 inch thickness and cut out with 1/2 inch star shaped cookie cutter. Place the cookies on the cookie sheets about 1 inch apart.
Place the 1/3 cup reserved egg white mixture in a bowl and add the lemon juice. Stir by hand until it is smooth. Brush the tops of all the cookies with this mixture to make a glaze. If it is too thick, add a few more drops of lemon juice. Bake for 20 to 25 minutes or until light brown and soft in the middle. Remove to cool on wire racks.

EASY COCONUT MACAROONS

Macaroons are a French delicacy and this is the easy way to make them. The recipe makes about 12 cookies and they are great for special occasions.

Ingredients:
1 (14 ounce) can sweetened condensed milk
2 teaspoons vanilla
2/3 cup all-purpose flour
5-1/2 cups flaked coconut
1/8 teaspoon salt

Directions:
Preheat your oven to 350 degrees and cover cookie sheets with foil (shiny side up) or parchment paper.

Place the condensed milk and vanilla in a large glass measuring cup and whisk to combine. Place the flour, coconut and salt in another bowl and whisk it up. Hand mix the flour mixture into the milk mixture. When it gets stiff, use your hands to knead everything in. Once it is well blended scoop out enough dough to create a golf ball sized ball and place them 2 inches apart on the prepared cookie sheets.

Bake for 12 to 15 minutes or until the coconut toasts. Remove to cooling racks and store in an air tight container once the cookies are cool.

CRANBERRY ORANGE COOKIES

These cookies will get your taste buds jumping with the tart and sweet flavor of cranberries and orange. This recipe makes 48 delicious cookies with a luscious frosting over top.

Ingredients:
2-1/2 cups all-purpose flour
1/2 teaspoon baking powder
1/4 teaspoon salt
1 cup softened butter
1 cup granulated sugar
1/2 cup brown sugar packed tight
1 egg
1-1/2 teaspoon orange zest
2 tablespoons orange juice from a real orange
2 cups chopped fresh cranberries
1/2 teaspoon more orange zest
3 tablespoons more of orange juice
1-1/2 cups confectioners' sugar

Directions:
Preheat the oven to 375 degrees and prepare cookie sheets by covering with parchment paper.

Whisk the flour, baking powder and salt in a large bowl and set aside. Cream the butter, granulated sugar and brown sugar in the mixture until it is smooth. Beat in the egg and then mix in the 1-1/2 teaspoon of orange zest and 2 tablespoons orange juice. Gradually add the flour mixture until it is all incorporated. Add the cranberries and mix by hand. Scoop out rounded tablespoons of the dough and drop them on the cookie sheet about 2 inches apart. Bake for 12 to 14 minutes until edges turn golden. Remove to cool on wire racks.

Once cool make the frosting in a medium sized bowl by combining the 1/2 teaspoon orange zest, 3 tablespoons orange juice and the confectioners' sugar. Mix well by hand until it is very smooth. Spread over the tops of the cooled cookies and let stand until the icing gets hard.

CARAMEL CHOCOLATE COOKIES

In this cookie you wrap the dough around caramel filled chocolate candy. They are extremely decadent and full of calories, but once a year they make for a wonderful snack. This recipe makes 24 cookies that won't last long at all.

Ingredients:
2-1/4 cups all-purpose flour
1 teaspoon baking soda
3/4 cup unsweetened cocoa powder
1/8 teaspoon salt
1 cup softened butter
1 cup granulated sugar
1 cup brown sugar packed tight
2 eggs
1 cup chopped nuts
1 more tablespoon granulated sugar
48 chocolate covered caramel candies, unwrapped

Directions:
Whisk together the flour, baking soda, cocoa powder and salt in a large bowl and set aside. Cream the butter and both sugar in a mixer until soft and fluffy. Add the eggs and beat well. Add the flour mixture gradually to the butter mixture until it is all incorporated. Stir in half of the chopped nuts by hand. Cover the bowl and chill in the refrigerator for about 1 hour.

Preheat the oven to 375 degrees and cover cookie sheets with parchment paper.

Divide the dough into 4 sections. Take one section and put the rest back in the refrigerator. Divide this section into 12 pieces and quickly press the piece around one of the chocolate covered caramel candies. Roll into a ball, Place the other half of the nuts and the 1 tablespoon sugar in a bowl and dip the top of the ball into this mixture. Place, sugar side up, on the cookie sheet 2 inches apart. Continue with the other pieces of dough and candies.

Bake for 8 minutes. Cool 5 minutes on the cookie sheet and remove to wire racks to cool completely.

MINT MERINGUES

These cookies are sometimes also called divinity and you can make them several different ways. My favorite is peppermint types with the dough dyed pink or light green. This recipe makes 48 cookies that are light and crunch when you bite into them and are air filled and delicious inside.

Ingredients:
2 egg whites
pinch of salt
1/8 teaspoon cream of tartar
1/2 cup granulated sugar
2 candy canes that have been crushed.

Directions:
Preheat the oven to 225 degrees (no higher) and line cookie sheets with parchment paper.

Use only a glass or metal bowl that has been put into the refrigerator to cool. Beat the egg whites with an electric mixer with the salt and cream of tartar until it starts to form soft peaks. Gradually add the sugar until form peaks form. Scoop out dough, which should be very light and airy, by teaspoonfuls and drop on cookie sheets 1 inch apart. Sprinkle with crushed candy cane.

Bake for 1-1/2 hours. They should not be brown but should be dry on the inside. You may just have to ruin one or two to break them open to see if they are done. Eat the evidence. Turn off the oven immediately and leave the door open a little so it will cool off quickly. Let them sit in the oven until they are cool. Use a metal spatula to get them loose from the parchment paper and store in an air tight container.

Variations: Add one or two drops of food coloring to color the cookies. You can also fold in about 1/2 cup of mini chocolate chips for a chocolate mint treat. Make the meringues different flavors by adding a few drops of anise, orange, lemon or vanilla flavoring.

NO BAKE CHRISTMAS WREATH COOKIES

This recipe is for a no bake cookie made with cornflakes and marshmallows dyed green with food coloring and red hots as the decoration. They are actually shaped in wreath shapes. This recipe makes 18 cookies that must be stored in an air tight container.

Ingredients:
1/2 cup butter
30 large marshmallows
1 to 1-1/2 teaspoons green food coloring
1 teaspoon vanilla
4 cups cornflakes
2 tablespoons of red hot cinnamon candies

Have ready some cookie sheets covered with wax paper.

Place the butter in a large saucepan over medium heat and melt. Drop the marshmallows in and stir constantly until they melt so they do not burn on the bottom or sides of the pan. Remove from the heat and add the food coloring. You want a bright green color. Also add the vanilla and stir in well. Add the cornflakes and start stirring so that they are all coated with the butter mixture.

You have to work quickly while the mixture is still warm or you will never get everything to stick together. Drop a heaping tablespoon of the mixture on the wax paper and form it into a wreath with a hole in the middle. Lightly grease your fingers with butter to do this and be careful because it will be a little hot. Press in about 4 to 5 red hots around the wreath to decorate it. Let the wreaths cool to room temperature.

EGGNOG COOKIES

If you like eggnog, you will love these cookies. They have the spicy flavor in the cookie and in the icing. This recipe makes 72 cookies and they do freeze well.

Ingredients:
3-1/4 cups all-purpose flour
1 teaspoon baking powder
1 teaspoon baking soda
1/4 teaspoon salt
1 cup softened butter or margarine
1 cup granulated sugar
1 egg
1 cup eggnog
1-1/2 cups confectioners' sugar
3 tablespoons more of eggnog

Directions:
Preheat your oven to 350 degrees F and cover cookie sheets with parchment paper lightly sprayed with non-stick spray.

Place the flour, baking powder, baking soda and salt in a large bowl and whisk to combine. Set aside. Place the butter and granulated sugar in your mixer bowl and cream on high until it is very smooth. Add the egg and beat well. Gradually add the eggnog alternately with the flour mixture until it is all combined into a soft and gooey dough. Drop by teaspoonfuls on the cookie sheets about 1 inch apart

Bake 8 to 10 minutes and remove from oven and let cool on the baking sheet 5 minutes before removing to a wire rack. Cool completely before making the icing.

Place the confectioners' sugar in a small bowl. Add 1 tablespoon of eggnog and stir to combine. Add the other 2 tablespoons stirring after each addition. You may or may not need all of the last tablespoon. The icing needs to be spreadable, so don't make it too thin. If you do, just add a little more confectioners' sugar. Spread over the cooled cookies and let the icing harden before storing in an air tight container.

PINK PEPPERMINT BALLS

Who doesn't like the refreshing flavor of mint for a winter holiday? These Peppermint balls are essentially a butter ball recipe with added peppermint and pink color. The recipe makes 60 cookies that will freshen your breath too. Serve them after a heavy meal because mint helps your body process heavy, fatty foods.

Ingredients:
3 cups all-purpose flour
1 teaspoon baking powder
1/4 teaspoon salt
3 cups confectioners' sugar, divided
1-1/4 cups softened butter
1 teaspoon peppermint extract
1 teaspoon vanilla
1 egg
pink food coloring
1 cup finely crushed candy canes, divided
1 cup granulated sugar
3 tablespoons milk

Directions:
Preheat the oven to 350 degrees F and line cookie sheets with parchment paper sprayed with a little non-stick spray.

Whisk together in a bowl the flour, baking powder and salt and set aside. Place 1-1/2 cups of the confectioners' sugar and butter in your mixer and cream until it becomes smooth. Add the peppermint extract, vanilla, egg and food coloring and beat until smooth. If you cannot find pink food coloring, use a tiny bit of red to just tinge the dough with a pink color. You should be able to find pink food coloring at hobby stores in with the cake decorating equipment. Gradually add the flour mixture until everything is blended and a stiff dough forms. Remove from the mixer and hand stir in half of the crushed candy canes. Reserve the other half for later.

Place the granulated sugar in a small bowl and roll the dough into 3/4 inch to 1 inch balls and roll them in the sugar before placing them 1 inch apart on the cookie sheets. Bake about 10 to 12 minutes or until pinkish brown. Remove from the cookie sheets and place on cooling racks to cool completely.

Make a glaze by mixing the other 1-1/2 cups confectioners' sugar with the milk until smooth. It should be thin enough to drizzle over the cookies. Sprinkle with the rest of the crushed candy cane. Let the glaze harden before placing in an air tight container.

LEBKUCHEN

Lebkuchen was made as early as the late 1200s by monks in Nuremberg, Germany and is a cross between gingerbread and fruit cake. The precursor to this treat was the honey cake. This recipe makes 12 bars.

Ingredients:
2 cups all-purpose flour
1/2 teaspoon baking soda
1 teaspoon baking powder
1-1/3 cups honey
1/3 cup brown sugar packed tight
1 cup chopped candied fruit
1 tablespoon sesame oil
1/4 teaspoon ground ginger
1/2 teaspoon ground cardamom
2 teaspoons ground cinnamon
1/4 teaspoon ground nutmeg
1-1/2 cups more flour
candied cherries and whole almonds for decoration

Directions:
Preheat your oven to 325 degrees and spray a 10 by 15 inch baking pan with non-stick spray.

Whisk together the flour, baking powder and baking soda and set aside. Microwave the honey and brown sugar in a 4 cup glass measuring cup and stir after 1 minute on high. It should be melted and smooth. Pour into a large bowl. Add the flour mixture mixing in by hand until well combined. Stir in the candied fruit, sesame oil and all the spices.

Place the dough on a floured board and knead in the 1-1/2 cup more of flour to make a very stiff dough. Spread it into the pan evenly. You will be cutting into 12 bars once the dough is cooked, so figure out where the cuts will be and decorate each bar with a cherry in the center and four almonds coming off like rays of the sun. Bake for 20 minutes or until you can push a toothpick in the center and it comes out clean.

Cut into the 12 bars and wrap in plastic wrap and then in foil. Store in the refrigerator for about 1 week before serving. If you would like, glaze with a confectioners' sugar, milk and vanilla glaze before serving.

OLD TIME ANISE SPRINGERLE COOKIES

I had a friend whose mother made these every Christmas. Because they need to dry for several hours, the house always smelled spicy and delicious when she made them. These cookies are very hard and should be dunked in something before eating. They have a very strong flavor and most of the time have designs on the top made by carved rolling pins or wooden molds pressed into the dough. This recipe makes 46 cookies.

Ingredients:
1-1/2 tablespoons crushed anise seed
4 eggs
2 cups granulated sugar
1/2 teaspoon anise flavoring
3-1/2 cups all-purpose flour
1 teaspoon baking powder
1/4 cup confectioners' sugar

Directions:
Cover about 5 or 6 cookie sheets with parchment paper and sprinkle evenly with the anise seed. To crush the anise seed, use a mortar and pestle or sandwich between wax paper and roll with a rolling pin.

Place the 4 eggs and granulated sugar and anise flavoring in your mixer bowl and beat until it is frothy for about 6 to 8 minutes. Whisk together the flour and baking powder and slowly add it in to the egg mixture until well combined making a stiff and thick dough.

Roll the dough out on a confectioners' sugar covered surface until 1/4 inch thick. Lightly dust with more confectioners sugar and place a wood mold over top and press down until the design is transferred to the top of the cookie. Take a small sharp paring knife and cut a frame all around the design. Do for all the cookies. If you do not have molds you can just cut the frame and a cross in the center. Scoop up each cookie with a metal spatula and place on the prepared cookie sheets. The anise seed with adhere to the back of the cookie. Place the cookie sheets somewhere where they will not be disturbed and place a clean kitchen towel over the them. They need to dry out for at least 8 hours or overnight.

Preheat the oven to 250 degrees F and bake the cookies about 25 to 30 minutes or until they turn a very pale gold. Cool on cooling racks and store in airtight containers.

HOT CHOCOLATE COOKIES WITH MARSHMALLOWS AND CANDY CANES

These are probably my favorite holiday cookie. They are cooked and the marshmallows are placed on top afterwards so they do not melt. They actually do taste like hot chocolate with peppermint sticks. This recipe makes 60 cookies and you cannot freeze these because of the raw marshmallows.

Ingredients:
2 cups all-purpose flour
3/4 cup hot chocolate mix (the type you get in the round box and make many hot chocolates from)
1 teaspoon baking soda
1/4 teaspoon salt
1 cup softened butter
2 cups granulated sugar
2 eggs
1 teaspoon vanilla
1 teaspoon almond extract
1-1/2 cups chopped white chocolate
12 candy canes crushed
1 (10.5 ounce) package mini marshmallows

Directions:
Preheat your oven to 350 degrees and cover baking sheets with parchment paper.

Whisk together the flour, hot chocolate mix, baking soda and salt in a bowl and set aside. In your mixer, beat the butter and sugar until it is well creamed and add the two eggs, vanilla and almond extract. Mix until smooth and then add the flour mixture gradually until it is well blended and forms a soft dough. Add the white chocolate and hand fold it in to the dough.

Drop by rounded teaspoonfuls on to the cookie sheets about 2 inches apart. Sprinkle liberally with the crushed candy cane and bake for 8 to 10 minutes or until the edges brown a little. Remove from oven and immediately place mini marshmallows on top so they melt a little on the cookie. Cool completely and store in an air tight container.

Italian Wedding Cookies

If you go to a real Italian wedding, you will see they have a cookie table set up with thousands of cookies to be eaten and the reception along with the cake. One of those cookies will be a round cookie toped with a colored frosting that has a strong anise flavor. These are Italian Wedding cookies and they work well for any special occasion including the holidays. You can also make them orange and lemon or orange flavored. This recipe makes 40 cookies. You might want to double it.

Ingredients:
2-1/2 cups all-purpose flour (You may need more, up to 3 cups)
1 tablespoon baking powder
1/2 cup softened butter

1/2 cup granulated sugar
3 eggs
2 teaspoons anise extract
2 to 3 tablespoons milk
2 cups confectioners' sugar
3 tablespoons milk
1/2 teaspoon more anise extract
food coloring

Directions:
Preheat your oven to 350 degrees and line cookie sheets with parchment paper.

Whisk together the flour and baking powder in a large bowl. Use only the 2-1/2 cups flour until you think you might need more. Set aside. Cream the butter and sugar in your mixer until smooth. Add the eggs, mixing well after each one. Add the anise extract and beat in. Add 1/3 of the flour mixture to the butter mixture and beat in adding 1 tablespoon of the 2 to 3 tablespoons of milk. Mix in another third of the flour and another tablespoon milk. The dough should resemble a thick browning mixture, so if you think you need to add more flour after adding the last batch of flour mixture and milk; do so. It should be softer than drop cookies.

Scoop out the dough and form into balls. (Use a cookie scoop to make it a perfectly round ball.) Place about 1 inch apart on the cookie sheets. Bake for 10 to 12 minutes. They should not be brown, but will be like a cake and soft inside. Remove from cookie sheets and let cool completely.

To make the icing, mix the 2 cups confectioners' sugar with the milk by hand. Add the anise extract and enough food coloring (any color) to tint the icing. Hold each cookie in your fingers upside down and dip the top in the icing turning it as you remove it from the icing. Place on cookie sheets and let the icing harden over night before storing in air tight containers. These cookies freeze well.

Variations:
Instead of adding anise flavoring, add orange or lemon flavoring and 1 teaspoon of orange or lemon zest to the cookie with the butter and sugar. Instead of using milk in the icing, use lemon or orange juice and sprinkle with some lemon or orange zest. Make the cookies almond flavored using almond flavoring in both the cookie and the icing. These cookies are great for weddings, Christmas and for Easter because you can make them elongated to look like eggs with pastel icing.

PIZZELLES

A pizzelle maker is essential to making these cookies. It is like a shallow waffle maker that puts a design on the cookie, which is usually round with designs etched into them. They are light and airy and you can make them in many different flavors. This recipe makes about 30 pizzelles depending on the size of your maker.

Ingredients:
1-3/4 cups all-purpose flour
2 teaspoons baking powder
1/2 cup melted butter
3/4 cup granulated sugar
3 eggs
2 tablespoons vanilla

Directions:
Whisk together the 1-3/4 cup flour and baking powder together in a bowl and set aside. Place the melted butter and sugar in the mixer and beat until creamed. Add the eggs and vanilla and beat well. Gradually add the flour mixture until well combined. The dough should be soft but not runny.

Drop the batter by rounded spoonful's onto the preheated pizzelle maker and close the lid. Cook for about 90 sections or until the steam stops coming from between the lid and bottom. The pizzelle should be lightly browned. Remove with a fork or chop stick and lay flat. They will harden as the cool.

Store in airtight containers at room temperature. This cookie should never be frozen.

Variations:
Anise – Add anise flavoring instead of vanilla
Almond – Add almond flavoring instead of vanilla
Lemon – Add lemon juice instead of vanilla and 1 teaspoon of lemon zest
Chocolate – Use 1 cup all-purpose flour instead of 1-3/4 cup and 1 teaspoon baking soda instead of 1-1/2 teaspoon. Add 3/4 cup unsweetened cocoa powder.
Gelatin flavors – Orange, Lime, Grape, etc. Use 1 small package of dry flavored gelatin (not the diet kind) instead of sugar and proceed with a matching extract. You can use orange or lime extract for those flavors and stick to vanilla with the grape. You can also add some food coloring to any pizzelle to make it another color.

Conclusion

I hope this book was able to help you to become the best cookie baker in town and that all your friends and family will look forward to getting delicious treats from you.

The next step is to start baking and trying the over 100 cookie recipes in this book. Make them for your family, friends, neighbors, coworkers, and get to know everyone by taking a plate of cookies over to thank them for something they did for you, for moving into the neighborhood, as a general gift or just because you think they need a plate of cookies. Make some cookies to send to our armed forces or a college student studying far away to make them feel more at home. The recipes in this book are old recipes, new recipes, recipes with a twist, unusual recipes, and recipes from all over the world. There is surely something to make a good day for anyone.

Finally, if you discovered at least one thing that has helped you or that you think would be beneficial to someone else, be sure to take a few seconds to easily post a quick positive review. As an author, your positive feedback is desperately needed. Your highly valuable five star reviews are like a river of golden joy flowing through a sunny forest of mighty trees and beautiful flowers! *To do your good deed in making the world a better place by helping others with your valuable insight, just leave a nice review.*

My Other Books and Audio Books
www.AcesEbooks.com

Popular Books

Be sure to check out my audio books as well!

 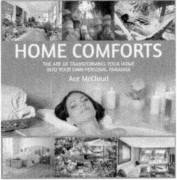 
  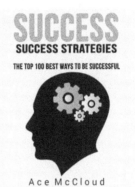

Check out my website at: **www.AcesEbooks.com** for a complete list of all of my books and high quality audio books. I enjoy bringing you the best knowledge in the world and wish you the best in using this information to make your journey through life better and more enjoyable! **Best of luck to you!**

www.ingramcontent.com/pod-product-compliance
Lightning Source LLC
LaVergne TN
LVHW081204050225
803024LV00014B/1048